THE VISITOR'S GUIDE
THE SEVERN
and
AVON

Visitor's Guide Series

This series of guide books gives, in each volume, the details and facts needed to make the most of a holiday in one of the tourist areas of Britain and Europe. Not only does the text describe the countryside, villages, and towns of each region, but there is also valuable information on where to go and what there is to see. Each book includes, where appropriate, stately homes, gardens and museums to visit, nature trails, archaeological sites, sporting events, steam railways, cycling, walking, sailing, fishing, country parks, useful addresses — everything to make your visit more worthwhile.

Other titles already published or planned include:
The Lake District (revised edition)
The Chilterns
The Cotswolds
North Wales
The Yorkshire Dales
Cornwall
Devon
East Anglia
Somerset and Dorset
Guernsey, Alderney and Sark
The Scottish Borders
  and Edinburgh
The Welsh Borders
Historic Places of Wales
The North York Moors, York and
  the Yorkshire Coast
Peak District (revised edition)
South and West Wales
Hampshire and the Isle of Wight
Kent
Sussex
Dordogne (France)
Brittany (France)
Black Forest (W Germany)
The South of France
Tyrol (Austria)
Loire (France)
French Coast
Iceland
Florence and Tuscany (Italy)

KEY FOR MAPS

	Towns/Villages
	Motorways
	Mainroads
	Rivers
	Lakes/Reservoirs
	Railways
𝔐	Museum/Art Gallery/Centre
𝛑	Archaeological Site
	Castle/Fort
	Ecclesiastical Building
	Building/ Country Park
	Cave
	Zoo
✳	Other Place of Interest
	Nature Reserve – Safari Park

The Visitor's Guide to
The SEVERN and AVON

Lawrence Garner

MOORLAND PUBLISHING

HUNTER
PUBLISHING INC

British Library Cataloguing in Publication
Data

Garner, Lawrence
    The visitor's guide to Severn and Avon.
    1. Severn River, Region (Wales and
    England) — Description and travel —
    Guide-books
    I. Title
    914.23'904858   D A670.S29

Published by
Moorland Publishing Co Ltd,
8 Station Street,
Ashbourne, Derbyshire,
DE6 1DE England.
Tel: (0335) 44486

ISBN 0 86190 148 7 (paperback)
ISBN 0 86190 149 5 (hardback)

Published in the USA by
Hunter Publishing Inc,
300 Raritan Center Parkway,
CN94, Edison, NJ 08818

ISBN 0 935161 19 8 (paperback)

Printed in the UK by
Butler and Tanner Ltd,
Frome, Somerset.

Black and white illustrations were supplied
by:
Frank Rodgers: 23, 25, 28, 31, 34, 37 (top),
39, 41, 43, 58, 91, 92, 96, 97, 101 (bottom),
103, 108, 112, 117, 127 (left); J.A. Robey 16,
17, 42, 59, 60, 100, 101 (top), 106, 110, 116,
121 (bottom), 122, 123; L.Porter: 18, 21, 36,
126, 138, 139; City of Bristol: 81 (top), 84, 85,
87, 92; SS Great Britain Trust: 84; Midland
Motor Museum: 29; Avoncroft Museum of
Buildings: 45 (top); Severn Valley Railway: 45
(bottom); Heart of England Tourist Board:
37 (bottom); Robert Opie Collection: 77;
YHA: 26; the rest of the photographs were
supplied by the author.
Colour illustrations were supplied by:
J.A. Robey (Avoncroft, Worcester, Upton-
on-Severn, Kenilworth, Warwick,
Charlecote, Welford on Avon, Coughton
Court); R. Scholes (Tewkesbury, Gloucester,
Wooton Wawen, Aston Cantlow, Alcester);
L. Porter (Ironbridge).

Contents

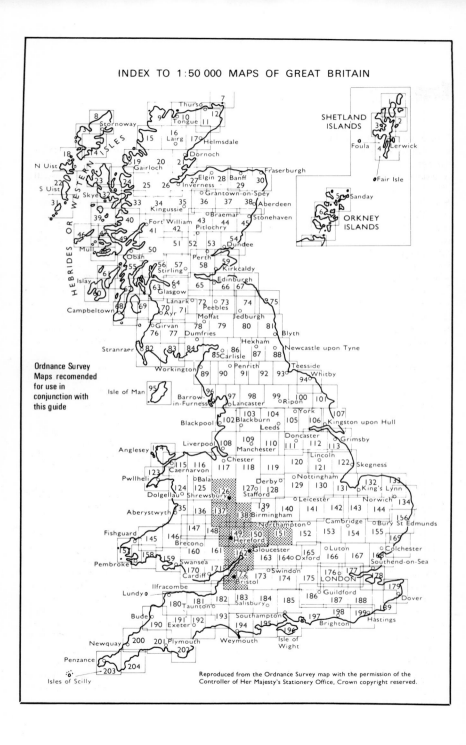

INDEX TO 1:50 000 MAPS OF GREAT BRITAIN

SHETLAND ISLANDS

ORKNEY ISLANDS

Ordnance Survey
Maps recomended
for use in
conjunction with
this guide

Reproduced from the Ordnance Survey map with the permission of the
Controller of Her Majesty's Stationery Office, Crown copyright reserved.

Introduction

There is a lot to be said for a holiday spent in following rivers. In themselves they create scenery that may be tranquil or exciting, but is seldom dull. Their effect on the lives of human beings has been profound, and the observant traveller is always conscious of the ingenious ways in which men have tried to use natural waterways to their own advantage, whether for energy, defence, irrigation, industry or transport. Riverside towns have an added dimension of interest and an enhanced visual attraction, and where bridges are few and far between the countryside flanking a river can remain remarkably unspoilt.

In the case of the Severn and Avon there are added attractions arising from the contrast between them. From the point where it enters England west of Shrewsbury the Severn grows quickly into a formidable river, simultaneously a threat and an asset. It has always been a great commercial waterway — in the early nineteenth century cargoes were being hauled well into Wales, and until quite recently there was heavy traffic between Gloucester and Stourport. Worcester and Gloucester still have port installations where you can sense the open sea not far downstream.

The Avon has none of this drama. True, it served a valuable commercial purpose at one time, but that is history. Nowadays it follows a placid course, linking quiet towns and watering some of England's most intensively cultivated countryside. It is essentially a civilised river passing through a lived-in landscape.

Between them the two rivers shape the area covered by this guide. It is a rough triangle that includes much of Warwickshire and Worcestershire, a substantial part of Shropshire and a strip of Gloucestershire. The corners of the triangle are Shrewsbury, Leamington Spa and Bristol — arbitrary choices perhaps, but limits have to be imposed and who is going to object to these three splendid towns?

Perhaps the first thing to be said about the region is that it provides a very happy balance between town and country. It comes as a surprise to find that this essentially rural area contains no fewer than three cities and nineteen major towns, all with distinctive characters and all worth exploring.

Some, of course, are already major tourist attractions. Warwick, Stratford-on-Avon, Worcester, Gloucester, Tewkesbury, Evesham and Pershore have for years been compulsory stops on tours of 'The Shakespeare Country' or 'The Green Heart of England', and it is high time that the rival claims of Shrewsbury, Bridgnorth, Ironbridge, Stourport, Bewdley and Upton-on-Severn were firmly stated. Bristol could provide enough interest for a week's holiday in itself.

And what of the countryside? There is little point in supporting the publicity-writers' pretence that it is all 'beautiful'. Some of it is dull and some of it is spoilt. The orchards and market gardens of the Vale of Evesham, for example, have little visual appeal except during the short-lived 'blossom time'. The northern areas of Warwickshire and Worcestershire have been under heavy commuter pressure for a long time, and the result has been not only insensitive modern housing but also the cult of the picturesque which can transform ancient and unpretentious villages into potential film sets. In many such villages signs of life are barely detectable.

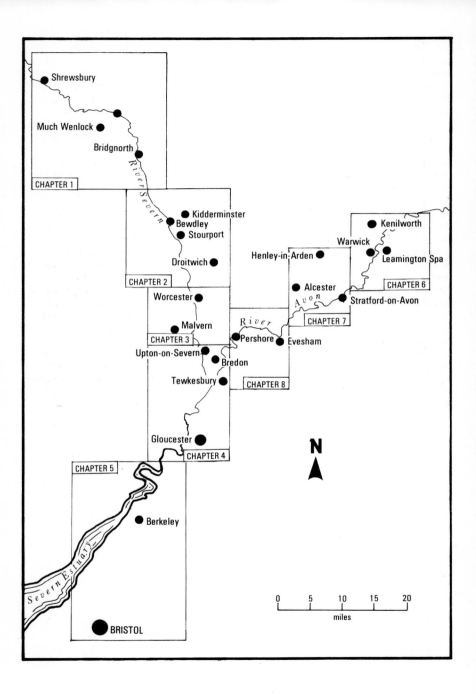

Shrewsbury

Much Wenlock

Bridgnorth

River Severn

CHAPTER 1

Kidderminster
Bewdley
Stourport

Droitwich

CHAPTER 2

Worcester

Malvern

CHAPTER 3

Pershore

Upton-on-Severn

Bredon

Tewkesbury

CHAPTER 8

Gloucester

CHAPTER 4

CHAPTER 5

Berkeley

Severn Estuary

BRISTOL

Henley-in-Arden

Warwick

Kenilworth

Leamington Spa

CHAPTER 6

Alcester

River Avon

Stratford-on-Avon

CHAPTER 7

Evesham

N

0   5   10   15   20
miles

Fortunately it is still possible to find genuine countryside away from 'the world of tweed caps and Hush Puppies, headscarves and retrievers, purring Jaguars and glossy geldings' as one writer has memorably described it. Along the shores of the Severn estuary, in Shropshire, in south and west Worcestershire a turn off the main road can lead to an unfashionable world of small, close-knit communities that know nothing of Best Kept Village competitions.

Suggestions for seeking out the best of the countryside are an essential part of this guide, which is written on the assumption that the average holidaymaker wants to squeeze a great deal of varied activity into a limited amount of time. For the same reason a basic itinerary of each town is included; they are not intended to replace the excellent 'town trails' that so many civic organisations now produce, but they will ensure that the visitor who has limited time, who finds the information centre unexpectedly closed or arrives in Stratford at 8am on a Sunday morning will be able to find the essential features of interest.

Other guides in this series have already covered the adjacent popular holiday areas — Somerset, south Wales, the Welsh borders and the Cotswolds — and this book follows the same format. Each chapter contains a subjective survey of a particular district, taking a fresh look at the well-known features and suggesting itineraries that include less famous but rewarding places. Occasional insets show outstanding attractions at a glance, and the final classified section is a comprehensive summary of what the area offers to visitors with a wide range of interests.

While the guide is written from the point of view of the land-based traveller it will obviously be of particular value to those planning a cruising holiday. The Severn is navigable for pleasure craft as far north as Stourport, and the Avon can be comfortably negotiated between Stratford and Tewkesbury. Canoeists, of course, have the freedom of both rivers.

Whatever the means of travel these two contrasting waterways and their surrounding countryside will provide the variety of experience that discerning visitors rightly seek.

1 Shrewsbury to Bridgnorth

Shrewsbury is the first English town on the river Severn. At a time when defence was a primary consideration it was inevitable that a settlement should grow up at this point, where the river describes a gigantic loop around a low hill and fails by only a few hundered yards to turn it into an island. With a castle sited to command the narrow strip of dry access security was as strong as it could be in the violent Saxon and early medieval period, when this border region rarely experienced a long period of tranquillity.

Inevitably Shrewsbury became a military headquarters and administrative centre with a stability denied to other towns nearby, and although it had its share of problems they were never serious enough to inhibit steady economic growth. By the end of the thirteenth century, the town was the natural market place for a wide area of surrounding countryside and was beginning to develop a wool trade that was to be its main source of prosperity.

As a result, there is no Shropshire town that has a greater wealth of early buildings at its centre, and only Ludlow can match its standard of later development, particularly during the eighteenth century. Much has been lost, of course, through random clearance and rebuilding even in recent times, but an early bypass built in the 1930s and a policy of putting old buildings to work for commercial purposes have ensured that Shrewsbury remains a town of enormous interest without being a museum piece.

Traffic in a constricted space remains a problem, and for the visitor wanting to park a car the best solution is to cross the Welsh Bridge on the west side of the town and use the big Frankwell car park just beyond it. A footbridge crosses the river from here and is a convenient start for a tour of the town.

Begin by walking along the river away from the Welsh Bridge, and after a quarter-mile climb the hill past a rather complicated traffic junction. On the left is the railway station, a very grand nineteenth-century imitation of a stately home or Oxford college, befitting Shrewsbury's former importance as a railway junction. A little further up the hill the impressive early seventeenth-century building on the right used to be Shrewsbury School, and the statue in front commemorates Charles Darwin, one of its most distinguished former pupils.

Directly opposite is a lane leading to the castle, which may prove something of a disappointment considering Shrewsbury's history as a military strongpoint. The earliest surviving remains are the eleventh-century perimeter walls and gateway. Edward I practically rebuilt the fortress in the late thirteenth century as a headquarters for his Welsh campaigns, and the Great Hall is the most substantial relic of that period. However, the castle now has a very civilised veneer as a result of Thomas Telford's remodelling in the late eighteenth century, when he converted it into a private house and thus paved the way for a distinguished early career as Shropshire's first County Surveyor.

After returning to the main street continue towards the Castle Street shopping centre, but note the lane turning off beside the big Presbyterian church on the left. It leads through an elaborately-carved Jacobean gateway into the courtyard of the old Council House, the meeting place of the Council of the Welsh Marches. The house has

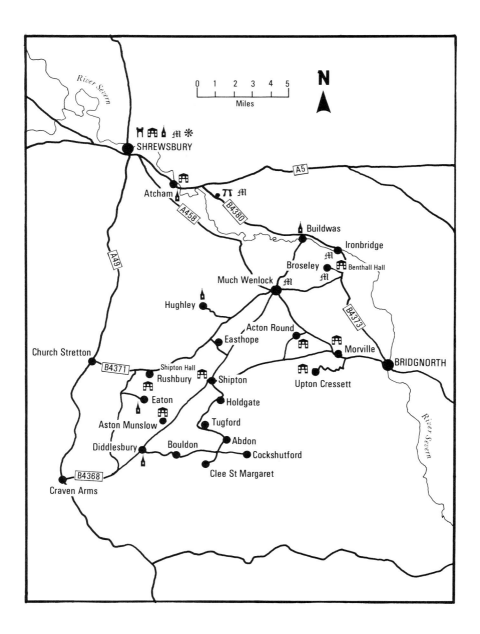

River Severn

0 1 2 3 4 5
Miles

N

SHREWSBURY

A5

Atcham

A458

B4380

A49

Buildwas

Ironbridge

Broseley

Benthall Hall

Much Wenlock

Hughley

B4373

Acton Round

Easthope

Morville

Church Stretton

B4371

Shipton Hall

Rushbury

Shipton

Upton Cressett

BRIDGNORTH

Eaton

Holdgate

Aston Munslow

Tugford

River Severn

Diddlesbury

Bouldon

Abdon

Cockshutford

B4368

Clee St Margaret

Craven Arms

been divided up and part of it was refaced in the eighteenth century, but a Jacobean porch marks the original entrance.

The big stores in Castle Street are the town's most obvious examples of nondescript modern development, but the shops on the other side of the road retain an interesting variety of styles and façades. The point where the traffic turns into St Mary's Street was the site of the High Cross, where Henry Percy's body was displayed after the battle of Shrewsbury to dispel rumours that he was still alive. From here there is a view down the pedestrianised Pride Hill, a shopping street that has kept much of its lively character in spite of new buildings and reshaped shop fronts.

Along St Mary's Street, the large church occupies a pleasant square. The spire can hardly be appreciated from here but it is one of the tallest in England. Basically Norman, the church has been extended and altered over centuries; one addition was the 1360 Chapel of the Drapers' Company, Shrewsbury's most powerful medieval guild. St Mary's is noted particularly for its rich collection of stained glass, much of it gathered from Europe by a nineteenth-century incumbent, although the fine east window was transferred here from the old church of St Chad which collapsed in 1788. St Mary's Place has on its south side the Drapers' Hall, built in the 1560s in affluent style with distinctively-carved timbers. The vast late-Regency building that looms to the east of the church is the former Royal Salop Infirmary, which replaced one of Britain's earliest public hospitals.

Across St Mary's Street and along Church Street is one of the town's most pleasant oases, St Alkmund's Place. The church on the south side retains its medieval tower but otherwise is a reconstruction of 1794, notable for a superb Georgian east window and for the use of cast iron in its nave windows. St Julian's church, just beyond it, has become redundant and is now a craft centre. The newly-restored group of buildings to the east is known as Bear Steps; and its outstanding feature is the fourteenth-century hall, used as an exhibition centre and normally open to the public — the roof timbers are particularly impressive. Butcher Row to the north is a most picturesque street, dominated by the finely-preserved Abbot's House at the top.

Behind the Bear Steps a steep and narrow alleyway (or 'shut' in these parts) with the graphic name of Grope Lane leads into the High Street, where The Square can be seen immediately opposite. This is the old heart of the town, where the market was held for centuries; the Tudor Market Hall still has its open ground floor and courtroom above. The statue is of Robert Clive, the Shropshire adventurer who enjoyed a meteoric career in India and returned to became MP for Shrewsbury in 1760. There is an interesting range of frontages on the north side of the Square but the most spectacular buildings in the vicinity are nearby in the High Street. Owen Owen's store now occupies Owen's Mansion, while the even more splendid Ireland's Mansion stands opposite. They are both superb examples of the sort of ostentatious town house that the late sixteenth-century wool merchants could afford to build.

Walk along the High Street in the other direction to the point where it narrows at the top of the hill. The busy road coming down on the left is Dogpole, which has its share of attractive buildings and is worth inspecting before continuing down the hill into Wyle Cop. The Lion Hotel on the right is of immediate interest. At first glance it seems to be a typically handsome coaching inn of the eighteenth century, but downhill from the main entrance is a small wooden balcony that indicates an earlier timber-framed structure. Just beyond it is the Henry Tudor House, a medieval shop with a fascinating upper window decorated with intricate tracery. Finally,

near the bottom of the hill, the imposing
Mytton's Mansion shows off its original
opulence at first-floor level.

Wyle Cop leads on to the English
Bridge and thence to Shrewsbury Abbey
on its island site. There was a Saxon
church here, but the important monastic
foundation was established by Roger de
Montgomery in about 1080. At the
Dissolution, the parishioners were
allowed to keep the church but the rest
of the buildings quickly disappeared, the
last remains being flattened when
Telford drove his Holyhead Road
through them in 1834, leaving only a
refectory pulpit standing on the far side
of the road. The massive tower was
added to the Norman nave in the
fourteenth century. Inside there is a
marked contrast between the simplicity
of this nave, with its huge pillars, and the
richness of the chancel which was
sensitively restored in the 1880s.

After returning over the bridge, the
road that branches to the left at the
bottom of Wyle Cop comes out on to the
town walls and into an area that is
mainly eighteenth century in character.
Below the walls, the riverside has been
reclaimed as a recreational space that
extends to the Welsh Bridge. The first
notable building on the right is E.W.
Pugin's Roman Catholic Cathedral of
1856, and not far beyond it, Belmont is
the first of several once-fashionable
streets leading down to the town centre
and providing an array of fine Georgian
architecture. The hospital on the left

13

St Chad's Church, Shrewsbury

strikes an uncompromising Victorian note in vivid contrast to the elegant vista that now opens up ahead as St Chad's church comes into view.

Standing on a prominent hill, St Chad's is the town's most striking church. The ruins of Old St Chad's can be seen at the bottom of Belmont. In 1788 Thomas Telford was called in to advise on its condition, and he made himself unpopular by pronouncing it to be on the point of collapse. His report was ignored but shortly afterwards it did indeed fall down without warning. The task of building a new church was entrusted to George Steuart, who produced an imaginative design comprising a three-decker tower with cupola and entrance portico, with an antechamber leading to a circular nave capable of seating 2000 people. The lightness and delicacy of the interior has been diminished a little by the addition of Victorian glass, but it is still a remarkable example of all that is best in eighteenth-century church architecture.

At this stage of the walk the park opposite St Chad's, known as the Quarry, will no doubt be a welcome diversion, affording the chance to sit by the river or to visit the charming garden created by Percy Thrower and called the Dingle. There is talk of reopening this upper part of the river to navigation (boats could once be hauled well into Wales) and such a move would restore to Shrewsbury the enlivening water traffic that is such a cheerful feature of Severnside towns further south. Not that there is a lack of activity on the water; Shrewsbury is a leading rowing school and this stretch is used for training. Some of the extensive buildings now occupied by the school can be seen up on the opposite bank.

The tour is concluded by walking down Claremont Hill on the far side of St Chad's, which emerges into busy Barker Street. By turning left Rowley's House, Shrewsbury's principal museum, is reached. It stands oddly amid a barren waste of bus station and car park, but nothing can detract from the impact of this large timber-framed house with a stone-built mansion grafted on at the back, and recent refurbishing has enhanced its appeal. It is a further short walk back to the Welsh Bridge and the Frankwell car park.

The journey down the Severn valley begins on the A5, and after only 2 miles the river reappears on the left and passes under the road at Atcham. Atcham is not much visited, presumably because its attractions lie off the road. By parking in the layby on the right just before the bridge, it can be seen that there are in fact two bridges separated by only a few yards. The 'new' one dates from 1929 and is a rather elegant, balustraded affair; the other, now closed to traffic, was built in about 1770 and has a much more rustic look. A 'Telford' milestone at its western end is the only indication that it once carried the Holyhead Road.

From the old bridge it is possible to admire the pleasing river frontage to the south provided by the mellow Georgian hotel and the sandstone church, which is the only one in the country dedicated to St Eata. Much of the north wall is Saxon work built with stones 'liberated' from the nearby Roman town of Viroconium. The dull exterior gives no indication of the riches inside. The east window, for example, is medieval glass, pale brown and gold, brought here from Bacton

church in Herefordshire. There is a Tudor window in the north wall commemorating a lady-in-waiting to Elizabeth I. The fine carving on the vicar's stall dates from the sixteenth century. The general impression is sombre, partly because of the inward-leaning walls and heavy roof timbers and partly because of a simple lack of windows.

On the other side of the main road is the impressive entrance to Attingham Park, one of Shropshire's greatest houses. Originally built between 1783 and 1785, it was altered by John Nash in 1807 but still retains its classical symmetry. Humphrey Repton landscaped the elaborate grounds. The house and grounds are now owned by the National Trust and are open to the public.

The A5 follows the park boundary for a long time before branching right on to the B4380 just opposite an old tollhouse. After half a mile watch out for a concealed car park on the right for visitors to the site of Viroconium.

The site looks small and a little unkempt, since excavation continues all the time, but what is seen on the surface is only a fraction of what remains to be unearthed. At its height, this was the fourth largest Roman city in Britain. Begun as a military camp in about AD50, it was developed as a civil town forty

Rowley's House, Shrewsbury

Attingham Park

years later for the benefit of the native tribal people, the Cornovii. After desultory progress, work was accelerated as a result of the Emperor Hadrian's visit to Britain in AD125, and one of the great finds here was a big inscribed tablet recording the dedication of the forum to the Emperor. Sophisticated archaeological techniques have detected various disasters, among them the collapse of the forum colonnade, the stumps of which can be seen on the sother side of the lane to Wroxeter. There is evidence that after the departure of the Romans, extensive wooden buildings were erected on the site, and a visit to nearby Wroxeter church will show that the stone was not wasted; the church gate boasts a Roman column on each side.

Most of the visible remains are of the extensive bath area and include a remarkably high section of wall. The site museum is fascinating. The more precious finds are in the Rowley's House

Museum in Shrewsbury, but equally interesting are the ordinary domestic objects shown here, including a meat cleaver and manicure set complete with nail file. Aerial photographs on display show, by means of crop marks, the outlines of whole streets, houses and defence works beneath the surface of the adjacent farm land.

The B4380 continues over a high plateau with a splendid view of the Wrekin on the left and the Welsh hills to the right. Another panorama opens up after the village of Leighton, when the road starts to run high above the Severn. Laybys provide a chance to stop and look at the river meandering dramatically below on its way to the entrance of the Ironbridge Gorge, marked by the cooling towers of a large power station. The next village is Buildwas, and to reach its famous abbey, take the next turning on the right towards Much Wenlock. The path to the abbey is 100yd past the river bridge.

Roman city of Viroconium, Wroxeter

It was founded in 1135 as a daughter house of Furness Abbey in Cumbria, and the original occupants were Savignacs (later Cistercians). The most substantial remains are of the church, with two finely-proportioned nave arcades and the east and west window spaces still intact. Of the other buildings the most impressive is the elaborately-vaulted chapter house floored with medieval tiles. It is a most tranquil spot, which seems to get few visitors. Just opposite the abbey's entrance path is the abrupt terminus of a railway line used to bring fuel to the power station. It once ran on to Much Wenlock and Craven Arms, and the former trackbed is still visible on the other side of the lane.

Continuing down the hill on the B4380, the immense cooling towers of the Buildwas power station begin to dominate the scene ahead. They are quite possibly the most awe-inspiring sight in Shropshire and certainly appropriate to an area once renowned for technological innovation — in fact the road signs here boldly proclaim Ironbridge as 'The Birthplace of Industry'.

It is probably no exaggeration to say that the course of civilisation was changed in this four-mile length of the Severn. The basic reason was the concentration in a small area of timber, coal, ironstone, clay and limestone, with the river as a convenient means of transporting heavy products over long distances: but these natural advantages might have counted for little without their exploitation by a few men of vision.

The mining of coal and the production of iron in charcoal funaces was already expanding when Abraham Darby I arrived here in 1708 from Bristol. He was in the business of making iron cooking pots, but he was obsessed with the possibility of making thinner sheet iron and much bigger castings. He chose a site in Coalbrookdale, a valley running north

Buildwas Abbey

from Ironbridge, and set about experimenting with the use of coke rather than charcoal for fuelling the furnaces. It was not an overnight breakthrough — several years passed before he was producing iron in large quantities by the new method — but the high quality of his product made possible developments that had been unthinkable before. The production of iron rails, for example, solved many transport problems and led to the rapid expansion of the industrial area.

It was Abraham Darby III who was responsible for the most spectacular pioneering achievement with iron. The lack of a river bridge had always been a problem, since coal and raw materials from Broseley on the other side had to be laboriously ferried across. The local ironmasters commissioned Darby to construct an iron bridge. Using entirely new engineering principles and making castings of an unprecedented size and weight, he completed the job in 1779. The bridge still stands, having given its name to the riverside settlement, and it has now become the symbol of the industrial achievements of the Gorge.

There were other achievements too. Telford came here to investigate the use of cast-iron for canal aqueducts, and the

eventual result was his remarkable structure at Pontcysyllte. Richard Trevithick's innovative steam locomotive was developed in Coalbrookdale. On the Broseley side of the river John Wilkinson first applied steam power to iron production and produced the world's first iron boat. At the other end of the Gorge a thriving ceramics industry developed. Two major firms of tile manufacturers emerged at Jackfield, while the famous Coalport works produced some of the finest china ever made.

Inevitably the depletion of resources and the rapid exploitation of the new processes in other parts of the country led to a decline in the Gorge's industrial activity. The works were run down or abandoned and the population moved to seek work elsewhere. Since no-one was interested in developing the area it remained fossilised, and there is hardly a building less than 100 years old. Thus in the 1960s the Ironbridge Gorge Museum Trust was able to set about creating the country's largest museum.

There is little point in describing the museum sites in detail since literature is so freely available, but it is worth pointing out that there is a composite ticket available for all the sites (the family ticket for parents and up to five children is a particular bargain) and the various portions can be used when desired. It takes at least two days to explore everything, and if only one site can be visited, the best choice is probably Blists Hill, which has a wide variety of exhibits in an open-air display, including a re-creation of a Victorian shopping street.

The following itinerary is suggested for those with limited time who want to catch the atmosphere of the Gorge.

On entering the town from Buildwas take the first major road to the left, signposted Coalbrookdale. The road passes several restored buildings, including the magnificent Coalbrookdale Institute, and at the top of the hill you can park at the Museum of Iron, where Abraham Darby's original blast furnace has been preserved inside a striking modern building. A short walk in this area provides a chance to look at the remarkable variety of buildings, with ironmasters' elegant houses and workers' cottages planted haphazardly together.

On returning to the riverside turn left and almost immediately right into the car park of the Severn Warehouse, an odd Gothic building that looks like a chapel. It houses displays introducing the Gorge and its history. From here it is a short walk to the iron bridge, along a waterfront that has changed very little — a random mixture of cottages, pubs and warehouses. The bridge is open only to pedestrians, and it is possible to get down to the river bank beneath it to study the elaborate castings used in its construction. The town's shopping centre is on the other side of the road, with a harmonious line of shops leading down to the wharf and an attractive square. The most prominent building here is the handsome Tontine Hotel of 1778.

As you look at the town from the bridge its character becomes clear. It is built on a steep slope, on which houses in a variety of styles and sizes perch, laid out in no discernable plan. A quick exploration can start with the climb to St Luke's church. It may be your only chance to walk under a graveyard, since the top section of the climb is a tunnel formed when the churchyard was built over the top.

To the west of the church a lane leads sharply downwards and will lead back to the waterfront. It provides unusual

The Iron Bridge

views of the houses below, and there are occasional glimpses of mysterious tracks leading off into the undergrowth. The idea of a preserved towns sounds artificial, but the Trust seem to take a pride in retaining the original appearance of their dwellings, including the grimy brickwork and waste spaces.

You should now drive past the bridge and take the Broseley road at the little roundabout. Very soon after, it is possible to park briefly to inspect the big 'Bedlam' furnace by the side of the road. Ignore the bridge to Broseley and continue along a surprisingly rural lane to a T-junction. A left turn here goes to Blists Hill open-air museum. Continuing to Coalport in the other direction, you will pass the Shakespeare Inn, beyond which is a roadside parking area. Stop here and go down one of the paths opposite the pub to reach the foot of the Hay inclined plane, a notable feat of engineering designed to haul boats bodily up and down between the two

levels of the canal. Here also is the Tar Tunnel (occasionally open) mined as a natural source of bitumen. The Jackfield footbridge gives access to the Tile Museum on the other side, while the canal towpath leads back to the Coalport China Museum.

To leave Ironbridge, return on the same road and take the Broseley road across the narrow bridge, which dates from 1908 and is of some interest as the first of any size to be constructed in reinforced concrete. On the other side of the river the road winds up adventurously with one very severe hairpin bend and enters the 'new' Broseley. Take the first on the right after the garage to reach the old town and park at the church entrance.

The church is Victorian, impressively battlemented and decorated with large gargoyles. It stands on the edge of a steep hill with wide views across the river, and although there is nothing outstanding about the interior it conveys

---

PLACES OF INTEREST IN AND AROUND IRONBRIDGE

Buildwas Abbey
Ruins dating from 1135, with substantial remains of church and notable chapter house.

The Iron Bridge
The world's first iron bridge, constructed by Abraham Darby III.

Museum of Iron
Displays illustrating the history of iron and steel making in Coalbrookdale. Exhibits include Abraham Darby I's blast furnace.

Severn Warehouse Visitor Centre
Explains the development of industry in the Ironbridge Gorge. Audio-visual displays.

Blists Hill Open-Air Museum
Extensive site with many reconstructed buildings and industrial workings.

Coalport China Works Museum
The original factory of the famous china manufacturers, now a museum showing production methods and a comprehensive display of Coalport china.

Jackfield Works and Tile Museum
Displays of decorative floor and wall tiles manufactured here from late nineteenth century to the 1960s.

Benthall Hall, Broseley
House basically of sixteenth century with noted plasterwork and panelling. Interesting church nearby.

Broseley Hall
Eighteenth-century house containing small museum relating to John Wilkinson, the outstanding Broseley ironmaster.

Severn Warehouse, Ironbridge

Ironbridge

The Guildhall, Much Wenlock

a sense of solidity and wealth. The adjacent Broseley Hall is occasionally open to the public and has a small museum relating to John Wilkinson, ironmaster and eighteenth-century 'king' of Broseley. Wilkinson's house, 'The Lawns', stands almost opposite the church with a prominent bow window which no doubt helped him to keep an eye on the main street. A walk further along Church Street and up into the shopping centre reveals a wealth of charming cottages and larger houses in a variety of appealing styles. The industrial grime has gone, and the little square could stand comparison with many a Cotswold village.

It is possible to reach Benthall this way (it is signposted about a mile out of town). The Elizabethan Hall is now a National Trust property, and the small church should not be missed. Although it stands in the Hall grounds it was not a private chapel; there was a sizeable settlement here until the population was drawn away to the nearby centres of industry. The sundial over the door catches the eye outside, and the immaculate interior has box pews, a fine gilded monument in the sanctuary and a dramatic modern painting by Edward Burra.

From here the road goes in to Much Wenlock, one of Shropshire's pleasantest small towns. Bypassed by the main road, its narrow streets are quiet and full of harmonious architecture. At the top end of the High Street beside the A458 is the extremely handsome Gaskell Arms, and the short walk back towards the town centre reveals several interesting buildings. Ashfield Hall has a stone ground floor supporting timber-framed upper works, while almost opposite a fine black and white house serves as Barclay's Bank. Raynald's Mansion is one of the county's best Tudor town houses, with a carved façade and tiny balconies between its three gables. At the heart of the town is the beautifully-preserved Guildhall, which still has its open ground floor and an upper room of great charm. The small but lively museum stands on the opposite corner.

The road from here to the Priory passes the parish church, of Norman origin but rather nondescript now. The severity of the Victorian restoration has been lightened somewhat by the recent refurbishing of St Milburga's Chapel in a striking contemporary style. Note also the memorial at the west end to Dr William Penney Brookes, a nineteenth-century athletics enthusiast and pioneer of the modern Olympic Games.

At the point where the path to the Priory branches off there is a group of very attractive old cottages, but the best blend of architecture in the town is in Shineton Street, which starts here. The range of houses and cottages in local stone have obviously been the subject of thoughtful conservation, and the unpretentious result is a triumph.

The ruins of the Priory are extensive and represent the third set of monastic buildings on the site. The original foundation took place in the seventh century, and 200 years later Leofric of Mercia rebuilt it. After the Conquest, Roger de Montgomery started the final ambitious scheme of construction, and it was during these works that the body of St Milburga, daughter of the first founder, was reputedly discovered 'sound and uncorrupted'. At the Dissolution, the Prior's lodging fell into private hands and remains intact today. Otherwise the ruins include substantial remains of the huge church, a finely-decorated chapter house and the well-head of the monks' lavatorium, which bears two fascinating pictorial carvings.

Priory Chapter House, Much Wenlock

23

Some of the finest and least-spoilt countryside in Shropshire lies to the west of Much Wenlock. It includes Wenlock Edge, Apedale and Corvedale, and is rich in tiny hamlets, deserted villages and traces of mining and quarrying associated with the Clee Hills. The area repays leisurely exploration on foot, but it is possible to catch much of its atmosphere in the course of an afternoon's drive. What follows is a suggested intinerary well off the beaten track.

Leave Much Wenlock on the B4371, which climbs directly on to Wenlock Edge. For the first 1½ miles the road runs between quarries producing the limestone that gives so many of the buildings in the area their distinctive look. Watch out for a concealed right fork after 2 miles. It leads to Hughley by way of a steep road through the thick woodland that blankets the Edge. Hughley is a good example of the many isolated hamlets in this part of Shropshire, consisting mainly of farms and associated cottages, with the occasional 'big house'. The buildings here are mostly of warm red brick, but there is one fine timber-framed cottage, all the better for having escaped 'restoration'. The church is notable for its fifteenth-century chancel screen with some medieval floor tiles behind it.

As you return to the B4371 you appreciate the massive, barrier-like appearance of the Edge, which looks almost insuperable from below. Turn right, and after less than a mile laybys on each side of the road provide a chance to park and walk to one of the best viewpoints, with a panaroma of thousands of acres of rich farmland, and the Wrekin rising sharply from it to the east. (Beware of letting children or dogs run ahead — at the time of writing the viewpoint is at the top of an unfenced precipice.)

Half a mile further on the Plough Inn marks a left turn down into Hopedale and the village of Easthope. (Walkers will note that 1 mile beyond the Plough is the start of a fine walk along the top of the Edge to Eaton.) Easthope is rather like Hughley in character but not in appearance, because here the cottages, barns and walls are built in the grey local stone. The church is isolated, but its site in the middle of lush green meadowland must be one of the most beautiful in the county. It was rebuilt after a fire about fifty years ago, but has been faithfully restored, with a new chancel screen made from ancient timber. Perhaps the most interesting feature here is under a yew tree on the north-eastern side of the churchyard: two graves, uninscribed but with plain crosses, lie side by side, reputedly the resting-places of two monks who died in a drunken brawl.

After turning round take the left turn at the junction near the church and rejoin the main road, which runs high and straight for two miles before emerging from the woodland and descending to Longville. After a further two miles look for an insignificant turn to Rushbury. A superb timber-framed house marks the outskirts of the village, and as you climb the hill to the centre there is an even better one on the left. Outstanding in a different style is the Old Rectory, a most ecclesiastical-looking building. Rushbury is a tranquil place, enlivened by the sounds of children in the little school, the oldest part of which dates from 1821. The interior of the church is a huge rectangle with no obstructions, made more imposing by heavy roof timbers.

Return to the road junction outside the village and turn left. The prominent hills ahead are part of the group to the east of Church Stretton. Turn left again opposite the farmyard just before the main road and drive for a little over two miles until you pass through the abutments of an old railway bridge that used to carry the line from Much Wenlock to Craven Arms. Just beyond it is Eaton, a picturesque cluster of buildings tucked away beneath the Edge and almost smothered by the thick woodland above. The church of St Edith is one of the most interesting in Shropshire, with a good deal of untouched Norman work and a floor that slopes sharply up towards the altar. The original roof timbers and chancel ceiling are particularly fine, as is the Jacobean pulpit and canopy. The effigy lying within the sanctuary dates from the mid-fourteenth century.

As you drive away from Eaton, take the turning on the left just before the railway bridge. This is the start of the most remote and attractive part of the tour, starting under the shadow of the Edge and then gradually climbing it through magnificent woodland and isolated hamlets. The route is via Harton and Westhope and then through Siefton Batch, a deeply-cut valley. The lane eventually joins the B4368, where you turn left and drive along a high road with views of Shropshire's most impressive range, the Clee Hills. Pass through Corfton and Diddlebury and on to Aston Munslow, turning left at the Swan Inn. A short distance up the lane is the White House, an interesting conglomeration of several architectural styles from medieval to Georgian. Opening hours are limited, but it is well worth a visit for its intrinsic interest as a dwelling and for its small museum of bygones.

It is now time to cross Corvedale to reach the Clee Hills, and the most direct route is through Diddlebury. The 'new' village lies beside the main road but the original centre is a few hundred yards down a side road, and very picturesque too with its stream and footbridge just below the church. This is very old indeed — its Saxon nave has herringbone masonry, there is a Saxon doorway, and the windows contain fourteenth-century glass.

Continue past the church and out into open country. Soon after crossing the river Corve, you pass some mounds in a field on the right, all that remains of Corfham castle, once strategically sited

Wenlock Edge, near Diddlebury

Wilderhope Manor Youth Hostel, Easthope, Much Wenlock

to command the valley route. Pass through Peaton and into Bouldon, where it is possible to park by the telephone box. Bouldon was once an industrial village, and iron was produced here until the 1790s. The site was then converted for paper manufacture and finally became a corn mill in the 1840s. You can reach the mill by walking up the lane that starts at the telephone box, although the result is not as rewarding as it might be because the iron waterwheel is now attached to a building converted in bijou style.

From Bouldon the lane contines uphill to Heath, where Heath Chapel, standing isolated in its field, is on the left. (If you want to go inside drive on about 300yd to the next farm for the key.) This is a famous church because the shell has been almost untouched since it was first built in the eleventh century. Its door, font and chancel arch are fine examples of primitive Norman work, while the pews and other woodwork date from no later than the seventeenth century. In the neighbouring field the traces of the medieval village which it served are still visible.

At the next crossroads go straight on towards Cockshutford. At the top of a short steep hill is a layby from which it is possible to climb Nordybank, the Iron Age hillfort nearby. This area is part of the old Clee Hills mining district and is notable for the squatters' settlements carved out of the common land by miners. A track leads east from Nordybank on to the hills, and by following the ridge northwards you can reach the 1700ft summit at Abdon Burf. A track beginning at 137: 591863 returns to the bottom of the hill, and the walk can be completed by way of the lane through Cockshutford.

From the layby turn back to the crossroads and turn left for Clee St

Margaret. The houses here have been
thoroughly restored and its most
interesting feature is the fact that one of
the village streets is the Clee Brook,
forming what is probably Britain's
longest ford. To the north of Clee St
Margaret is Abdon, a hamlet with an
unusual history: the original medieval
village became deserted and the place
was virtually re-colonised from the
seventeenth century on by miners. The
same thing happened at Tugford, $1\frac{1}{2}$
miles to the west, but here the squatters'
cottages built on the village green were
later demolished by order of the manor
court, which explains why the church
now stands alone in a field. There is a
fine Norman doorway here, and
fifteenth-century carving on the choir
screen.

The way out of Tugford is signposted
Stanton Long and runs across a high,
windswept plateau, reaching Holdgate
after 3 miles. This is another example of
a 'failed' village. Once a major
settlement, it now has only a motte and a
stone tower incorporated into a house as
reminders of its medieval importance.
The church has a notable Norman door
and font, and the plain nave (suffering
severely from damp) and uncluttered
chancel give it a spacious air.

Shipton is the last stop on this
itinerary. After passing through Stanton
Long and reaching the outskirts of the
village, go straight over at the first
crossroads and turn left at the next
junction to reach Shipton Hall. It is a
handsome building dating from 1587,
although the interior was altered a good
deal in the eighteenth century, being
equipped with iron fireplaces from
Coalbrookdale. The open space in front
of the Hall was created by clearing the
existing village when it was built,
although the little church was
undisturbed and now perches on a
nearby hill within the boundary of the
Hall grounds.

The B4378 out of Shipton leads back
to Much Wenlock, concluding a tour
that has taken in some of the
unfrequented countryside that typifies, if
anything can, the essential character of
Shropshire.

After leaving Much Wenlock for
Bridgnorth it is worth stopping at
Morville to walk down to the church and
survey the imposing façade of Morville
Hall, an eighteenth-century mansion in
grey stone flanked by substantial twin
lodges. It is a National Trust property

Market Hall, Bridgnorth

and can be inspected by written appointment. The church door has exceptional medieval ironwork on the door, and the font and chancel are arch are Norman. Four early wooden carvings of the Evangelists are placed at the top of the nave arcades.

And so into Bridgnorth, the most dramatic of the Severnside towns. From this direction you enter through solid suburbs, and to reach the town centre it is essential to drive straight on at the point where the main road turns sharply right. It is usually possible to park almost immediately on the left — advisable in fact because it is not easy to negotiate the town's narrow streets.

To understand Bridgnorth you need to stand at the centre of the bridge. On the west bank of the river High Town perches on top of precipitous sandstone cliffs, and it is easy to see why it was selected as a castle site early in the twelfth century. Below the cliffs is the waterfront, the source of the town's second lease of life in the sixteenth century. Here, and on the east bank, is Low Town, which acquired the railway

station and also much of the more recent industrial development. This very distinctive geography has ensured that High Town and Low Town have traditionally regarded themselves as independent communities.

The waterfront buildings are concentrated at the west end of the bridge, facing the landscaped remains of the wharves, and climbing away from them is a narrow street called the Cartway, for centuries the only way up the cliffs for wheeled vehicles. At the bottom it is impossible to miss Bishop Percy's House, a splendid sixteenth-century structure with decorated timberwork. Apart from his ecclesiastical career the Bishop is best remembered for his collection of traditional ballads called *Reliques of Ancient English Poetry,* a volume that brought new vision to poets at the end of the eighteenth century and certainly inspired Sir Walter Scott.

The Cartway rises steeply, passing some quaint buildings, including a cave in the rock that was inhabited until 1856, and emerges at the south end of the High

Street. The general effect of this wide thoroughfare is often marred by ranks of parked cars, but it is a pleasant, bustling shopping centre with many half-timbered buildings, notably the Swan Inn on the right. The Town Hall of 1652 is planted firmly in the middle of the street with traffic passing beneath it, and at the next crossroads Church Street leads off to the right towards the small 'close' surrounding St Leonard's church.

This is a very attractive place indeed. The church itself (closed at the time of writing) is Victorian, although its sandstone still looks remarkably new. Among the buildings grouped around it is the house occupied by Richard Baxter when he was a young curate here in the early 1640s and before he went on to become a controversial Puritan preacher and writer. The old Grammar School, looking rather dilapidated, stands isolated nearby. On the other side of the green is Palmer's Hospital, a group of almshouses built round a tiny courtyard, with three fine seventeenth-century houses almost next door.

Back in the High Street, the Northgate is the only survivor of the town's five medieval gates, although it has lost most of its character after extensive rebuilding. On the way back towards the town centre you pass Whitburn Street on the right, and a short way down is a very fine half-timbered pub called the King's Head. The Crown, at the corner of Whitburn Street, was once Bridgnorth's principal coaching inn.

There could hardly be a building less in keeping with its neighbours than the New Market at the south end of the High Street. Mid-Victorian, and constructed with bilious brick in Italianate style, it stands gloomily dwarfing the small-scale architecture around it. For a complete contrast cross the road into East Castle Street, Bridgnorth's most elegant road, where

Midland Motor Museum

PLACES OF INTEREST IN AND AROUND BRIDGNORTH

The Castle
The site of the castle, behind St Mary's church, is now a small park containing the remains of the keep leaning at a startling angle.

Bishop Percy's House
In the Cartway. Fine example of a substantial three-storied timber-framed house.

The Wharf
Landscaped area, once the site of important river port. Backed by sandstone cliffs with caves once used for storage and habitation.

Cable Railway
The only inland cable railway in Britain, and the steepest. Drops 200ft down cliff between High Town and Low Town.

Severn Valley Railway
Largest standard-gauge preserved railway. Northern terminus at Bridgnorth station, starting point for steam trips but also locomotive depot. Shop and refreshments.

Morville Hall
Morville, 3 miles west of Bridgnorth on A458. Elizabethan house with eighteenth-century additions. Magnificent frontage with fine flanking lodges.

Acton Round Hall
Off A458, 4 miles west of Bridgnorth. Early eighteenth-century mansion hardly altered since building.

Upton Cresset Hall
4 miles west of Bridgnorth. Elizabethan house with earlier Great Hall. Good interior decoration and interesting gatehouse.

Dudmaston Hall
At Quatt, 3 miles south of Bridgnorth on A442. Late seventeenth-century house, with notable furniture and pictures, including seventeenth-century flower paintings and modern pictures. Shop, refreshments.

Midland Motor Museum and Bird Garden
Entrance from Stourbridge road to east of Bridgnorth (Stanmore Hall). Outstanding collection of sports cars, racing cars and motor-cycles, with enthusiasts' shop. Extensive grounds containing lake and large bird garden.

---

the predominantly Georgian houses fit harmoniously together with a distinct atmosphere of wealth. Thomas Telford's church of St Mary Magdelene closes off the end in a fitting classical fashion.

Visitors are always guaranteed a shock on taking the path to the rear of the church and seeing the castle keep for the first time. It is a huge square block of masonry leaning at an incredible angle: the only substantial remnant of a Norman structure that once filled the site now laid out as a public garden. It can also be a surprise to hear the unmistakeable sound of a steam train, but Bridgnorth is the northern terminus of the restored Severn Valley Railway, and there is a good view of the station and yards from the parapet here.

To reach the railway it is necessary to get to the bottom of the cliffs. The short way is to go back past the keep and turn left on to a flight of steps at the bottom of which are two terraces of highly individual workmen's cottages in Ebenezer Row and Railway Street. The station entrance is immediately opposite. The longer way round via the town centre provides a chance to travel on Britain's only inland cliff railway — a convenient link between High Town and Low Town that has served a useful purpose since Victorian times. The descent brings you out on to the wharf, and the walk to the station passes some of the caves in the cliffs that were once storehouses and dwellings.

This rapid survey hardly does justice to a town that is full of surprises and has a centre hardly affected by contemporary development. It seems entirely fitting that the visitor should be able to leave on a train of the Great Western or London Midland, both of which are represented among the locomotives and rolling stock of the Severn Valley Railway.

The Severn Valley Railway started in 1965 as a small volunteer group, and by 1974 trains were running between Bridgnorth and Bewdley, a particularly attractive run that follows the river closely. In the course of twenty years a very large collection of engines, carriages and waggons has been acquired and restored, and the SVR is now the largest of the standard-gauge preserved lines.

Bridgnorth: Castle Ruins and Telford's church

2 Bridgnorth to Worcester

There is no road bridge over the Severn between Bridgnorth and Bewdley, and as a result the countryside between the two towns is remarkably unspoilt. The main road (A422) is quick and uneventful, though pleasant enough with its wealth of roadside woodland and frequent cuttings through the prevailing sandstone. On the way diversions are possible to the National Trust property of Dudmaston and to two Severnside villages.

Five miles from Bridgnorth there is a turning to the right for Hampton Loade, a slightly ramshackle settlement very popular with fishermen, where there is space to park beside the river and inspect the primitive cable mechanism of the passenger ferry. Four miles before Kidderminster, another right turn brings you to Upper Arley, a rather more interesting spot with a church, one or two pubs and a folly in the form of a fake medieval tower.

As you pass through the main road village of Alveley it may be surprising to see a substantial working-men's club in what seems to be a very rural spot. The club is the only reminder now that Alveley was once an outpost of the colliery that was centred at Highley on the other side of the river. On the approach to Kidderminster, the road swoops up and down dramatically, and the first sign of the town is a small and awkward roundabout at which some care is needed. Go straight on and follow the signs to the town centre where there is a multi-storey car park.

Kidderminster is not noted as a tourist attraction and by comparison with its neighbours Bewdley and Stourport it is an unattractive town. Its reputation, of course, is based on carpet manufacture, but its 'mill-town' character hides the fact that it was a very important textile centre from the thirteenth century onwards. The river Stour proved ideal for the fulling process, and Kidderminster achieved a reputation for cloth of great sophistication. It was not until the mid-eighteenth century that the first carpet loom was set up, and from that point the town began to take on the typical appearance of the Industrial Revolution, with functional mill buildings, huddled housing and numerous nonconformist chapels.

Nowadays a town centre of this kind would be jealously guarded by a civic society anxious to preserve its distinctive atmosphere, but there was apparently no-one to protest thirty years ago when much of the old town was flattened to accommodate a ruthless ring road and a gloomy pedestrian shopping precinct. The new road has isolated St Mary's church, which stands on a hill with the canal passing below it, and attempts to beautify the site serve only to accentuate the ugliness around it. It is worth visiting the church, however, to see the way in which it reflects the confident prosperity of the town in its heyday; there are some notable early memorials in the rich Victorian interior.

The view from outside the church includes several impressive factory buildings, and enthusiasts for industrial archaeology will want to explore what remains of the close-knit mill quarter. It is still possible to walk through streets that are more reminiscent of Lancashire than Worcestershire. But most visitors will find little to detain them, and more attractive surroundings can quickly be reached by taking the Bewdley road. There has been almost continuous housing development throughout this short distance, and the intervening

The Iron Bridge

Chainmakers' workshop, re-erected at Avoncroft Museum of Buildings

Worcester Cathedral

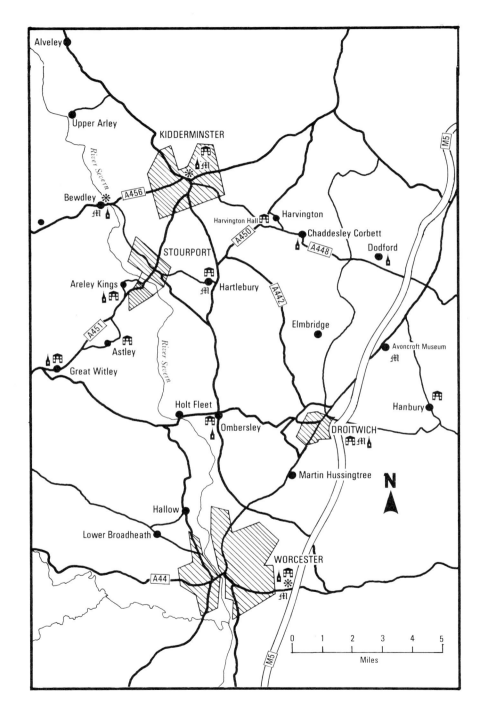

Alveley

Upper Arley

KIDDERMINSTER

River Severn

Bewdley A456

Harvington Hall
Harvington

A450
Chaddesley Corbett
A448
Dodford

STOURPORT

Areley Kings

Hartlebury
A442

Elmbridge

A451

Astley
River Severn

Avoncroft Museum

Great Witley

Holt Fleet
Hanbury

Ombersley

DROITWICH

Martin Hussingtree

N

Hallow

Lower Broadheath

A44

WORCESTER

M5

0 1 2 3 4 5
Miles

M5

village of Wribbenhall is now noticeable only as the site of the West Midland Safari Park, which occupies a former mansion and estate called Spring Grove. Bewdley is approached down a hill that has landed more than one vehicle in the river, and care is also needed to negotiate the sharp bend on to the bridge. To reach the car park drive into the main street and round behind the church.

The story usually told about Bewdley is that it was a flourishing town that went into sudden decline after its refusal to become the Severn junction of Brindley's Worcestershire and Staffordshire canal; the town authorities are supposed to have dismissed the new waterway as a 'stinking ditch'. In fact the decision was made on more considered grounds, and the main motive was understandable caution in the face of innovation, but the result was certainly a transfer of economic dominance to Stourport.

The prosperity of Bewdley came early. The nearby Tickenhill Manor was a royal palace under the Mortimers and for a time was the administrative centre of the Council of the Marches of Wales. A market was licensed early in the fifteenth century and borough status was achieved in 1472. In later years the town developed as a leading river port. Goods coming up the Severn from Bristol were distributed from here throughout the Midlands, and in the seventeenth and eighteenth centuries this privileged position gave Bewdley's own industries — mainly brass, horn and leather products — a considerable trading advantage.

The importance of the river in Bewdley's history is clearly seen from the bridge, designed by Thomas Telford and built in 1798. The older part of the town consists simply of a long waterfront with a compact commercial centre halfway along it. Load Street is more like a market square, closed off at

one end by the church and at the other
by the bridge. Nowadays this causes
problems because the much-used bridge
pours traffic straight into the town
centre and forces it to squeeze painfully
out at the other end.

The waterfront is undoubtedly the
finest in the Midlands — a harmonious
line of houses and shops in a variety of
styles spanning several centuries.
Severnside South, as it is rather
unimaginatively called, has the grand
buildings (those at the further end are
particularly fine) but the short terrace to
the north of the bridge is very attractive
in its own way and reminiscent of a
fishing village, although it was once a
coal wharf. The hire boats along here,
incidentally, are now moored to the
redundant ferry that used to ply at
Upper Arley, north of Kidderminster.

Load Street has a pleasing blend of
Georgian and Victorian architecture
with the occasional timber-framed
house. Halfway up on the left hand side
is the sandstone Guildhall of 1808 with
the old butchers' market occupying a
cobbled lane behind it. This Shambles
was purpose-built in 1783 with two
arcades to accommodate the stalls, and a
few years later three gaol cells were
added at the far end. In 1971 the
Bewdley Musuem Trust designed a
conversion, and it now houses displays
illustrating the old industries of Bewdley
and the Wyre Forest, local agricultural
methods and the history of the town
itself. There is space also for present-day
craftsmen to demonstrate their skills.
More recently an old brass foundry next
door has been reconstructed to explain
the history and techniques of the
industry with occasional practical
demonstrations. Other notable buildings
in Load Street are the George Hotel, a
former coaching inn almost opposite the
Guildhall, and the half-timbered
Bewdley Institute, which was also an inn
until 1877.

St Anne's church stands on an island
in the middle of the traffic. Its
seventeenth-century tower and
eighteenth-century nave and chancel
give it a curious hybrid appearance from
the outside, but inside it is spacious and
elegantly-proportioned. There are few
outstanding individual features, apart
from the unusual pastel-tinted glass of
its main windows.

Behind the church Park Lane leads
away uphill to Tickenhill Manor,
eighteenth century in style but
containing traces of the earlier building
that had royal associations. It has a
niche in history as the scene of the
marriage by proxy of Prince Arthur,

The Severn at Bewdley

Henry VIII's elder brother, to Catherine of Aragon in 1499. Back at the bottom of Park Lane a right turn brings you into High Street, where several buildings catch the eye. Almost immediately on the right is the richly-timbered Bailiff's House of 1610. The Manor House, a little further along, is of roughly the same date and stands opposite the Redthorne Hotel, once the home of Peter Prattington, a celebrated local historian of the eighteenth century.

The continuation of the High Street across the top of Lax Lane is called Lower Park and contains the early seventeenth-century Sayers Almshouses and a Friends' Meeting House of 1690, where the wife of Abraham Darby I is buried. Lower Park House was the birthplace of Stanley Baldwin, MP for Bewdley and Prime Minister during the Abdication crisis. The pleasant Lax Lane (thus called after the Danish word for salmon) runs down to the riverside and the distinguished range of buildings lining Severnside South.

While Bewdley has been content to grow old gracefully and without ambition, its neighbour Stourport has expanded aggressively, and it is difficult to detect any break between the tow towns. Stourport is reached by returning over the bridge and taking the minor road on the right almost immediately after, a route that passes the southern headquarters of the Severn Valley Railway. A long drive through ribbon development ends in a one-way system, and it is best to follow the signs for the riverside car parks where there is ample space for visitors.

Stourport is one of the few English towns created entirely as a result of canal engineering, and the fact that the canal era coincided with a period of fine architecture ensured that the town's original nucleus is a very attractive place. When Brindley was seeking an outlet for his Worcestershire and Staffordshire Canal in the 1770s the

obvious choice was the established port of Bewdley, but having been rebuffed in that quarter he set about building a port entirely from scratch at the hamlet of Mitton, 4 miles downstream. The central feature was a complex of basins and wharves, with warehouses, cottages and a large inn, all built in homogeneous style. The decline of the river and canal area brought a temporary desolation to the area, but luckily very little was lost, and in recent years Stourport has once again become a flourishing waterside community through the development of recreational boating.

Nowadays this is a favourite resort for Midlanders, and among the attractions for the day visitor are steamer trips and a small funfair. Anyone who prefers quiet exploration should avoid bank

The Canal Basin, Stourport

PLACES OF INTEREST IN AND AROUND BEWDLEY AND STOURPORT

Bewdley Museum
In the former Shambles, the museum is devoted mainly to local life and history, in particular the trades and industries of the district. Includes a working brass foundry and modern craftmen's shops.

Brass Rubbing Centre
Lax Lane Craft Centre, Bewdley. Replicas of medieval and Tudor brasses.

Stourport Canal Basins
Junction of the Staffordshire and Worcestershire Canal, constructed by James Brindley in the late eighteenth century. Much of the complex survives and is in use for pleasure craft. Original buildings include Tontine Hotel and range of offices and warehouses.

West Midlands Safari and Leisure Park
On A456 between Bewdley and Stourport. Impressive animal reserves and wide variety of amusements.

Severn Valley Railway
Southern depot is at Bewdley station. Frequent steam trains in summer between here and Bridgnorth, also model railway display, shop and refreshments.

Witley Court
On A443, 5 miles south-west of Stourport Grounds of remarkable mansion, now ruined. Also magnificent Baroque church of St Peter.

Wyre Forest
3 miles west of Bewdley. Visitor Centre, nature trails, deer.

add vitality and interest to a walk through the old canal terminal, which is situated to the east of the fine iron road bridge of 1870.

Walk beneath the bridge (note the unusual spiral staircase) and along the path that leads past the funfair. A hump backed bridge crosses the end of the lock that allows access for narrow boats from the river to the first basin. The roofed section just beyond the lock is a dry dock. The path continues to the barge lock, designed for the much larger trows which were hauled in here from the river for unloading. There is no bridge here — you have to cross the lock gates themselves, and the operation needs some care. The large brick building ahead is the famous Tontine Hotel, erected in the 1770s as a facility for merchants and boat-owners. From this point there is a view downstream of the 1928 power station, once regarded as an eyesore but now claiming the attention of industrial archaeologists.

Walk round the right hand side of the Tontine and into Mart Lane, which runs up the side of the upper basin and provides an excellent view of the wide variety of craft moored here against a background of one of the original dock buildings (now the Stourport Yacht Club) surmounted by an elegant clock tower. Towards the top of Mart Lane are some merchants' houses, and Lichfield Street, the turning to the right at the top, also has examples of these early dwellings.

The walk continues into York Street, reached by crossing Wallfield canal bridge with its interesting tollhouse. This is one of Stourport's original streets and contains a pleasing blend of modest Georgian frontages. From the crossroads at the end it is possible to return to the river down busy Bridge Street or to extend the walk in the other direction into the High Street. This shopping centre marks the transition between the old town and the later development to the north, and although many of the buildings have been adapted

holidays and summer weekends; on other days in the holiday season there is just the right level of boating activity to to modern commercial use there are still some good Georgian façades on the eastern side. A right turn at the top of the High Street leads past the Black Star, a canal-side inn, and another right turn into Lion Hill leads back to the Wallfield Bridge.

The main road from Stourport to Worcester is fast and convenient but lacking in interest for the visitor who wants to explore this north Worcestershire countryside. Two alternative routes are suggested here, and they can be combined into a circular tour.

The first begins on the A451. Cross Stourport bridge and almost at once look out for a right turn signposted Areley Kings Church. The village is now something of a commuter dormitory, but the church and its associated buildings have been left in isolated tranquillity on the top of a hill overlooking the Severn valley.

Architecturally the church is undistinguished inside or out, but it has a remarkable connection with Layamon, author of the early English poem *Brut*, written in about 1200. The poet's introduction to his work indicates that he was parish priest here, and the fact was confirmed in 1886 when restoration work unearthed the base of a font inscribed with his name. The font can now be seen in the church. The churchyard is notable not only for a fine view but for the buildings on its perimeter. The half-timbered Church House probably dates from the sixteenth-century styles and features something to be envied by every married man — a capacious garden house, built by the Rev Richard Vernon in 1728 as 'a retreat from domestic cares'. One final curiosity is the 'Coningsby Wall', a block of stone at the western edge of the churchyard. It was apparently inserted into the boundary wall of the churchyard at the behest of Sir Harry Coningsby, a member of the famous Herefordshire family, who retired here after accidentally drowning his son. Intended as his own memorial, it bears the inscription 'Lithologema quare: Reponitur Sir Harry', an eccentric trilingual declaration meaning 'Why a stone monument? Sir Harry Lies here'. He died in 1701 and the block was later moved closer to his tomb.

As you leave this pleasant place and continue towards Great Witley it is worth making a brief diversion to Astley reached by a turning to the left about 3 miles from Areley. Astley Hall was the home in later life of Stanley Baldwin, but less well-known is Andrew Yarranton, who was born at nearby Yarhampton in 1616. He was a pioneer in industry and agriculture well before the more famous innovations of the eighteenth century. He is credited with the introduction of clover and sanfoin into the Midlands and was also a canal fanatic, carrying out navigational

The Tontine Inn,
Stourport

improvements between Stourbridge and Kidderminster. A few years ago one of his experimental iron furnaces was excavated by the river bridge between Yarhampton and Astley.

Less than a mile south of Astley is Glasshampton monastery, founded as an Anglican community in 1918 and housed in the stable block of a mansion that was later destroyed by fire. The original founder, Fr William Sirr, failed to establish his order, although a good many social outcasts found refuge there, but the buildings were taken over in 1947 by the Society of St Francis. The monastery is reached by a public track at the bridge that carries the B4196 over the river.

Back on the A451 you pass beneath Abberley Hill to reach Great Witley. It is an indeterminate sort of village, and to find its big attraction it is necessary to leave again on the A443, and watch out after nearly a mile for an unobtrusive lane on the right, signposted Great Witley Church. One is not told that it is also the way to Witley Court, one of the most extraordinary ruins in the Midlands.

The original mansion was acquired by Thomas Foley, son of a wealthy ironmaster from Stourbridge, in the late seventeenth century. The family were ambitious to become landed gentry, a process that was accelerated in 1712 when Foley's grandson became a Baron. He devoted much of his life to extending the house, and his widow had the parish church rebuilt in 1735, attaching it to one end of the mansion and thus making it something of a private chapel. The last of the Foleys added an enormous portico before the estate was sold to the future Earl of Dudley in 1838. He too added his share of extensions. The end result was a vast, sprawling residence conforming to no known architectural style. When it was seriously damaged by the fire in 1937 it was left to disintegrate during the war, and only recently has a determined effort been made to save the church. The ruins of the house are now

being made safe, and at the time of writing access to them is prohibited. Visitors can, however, visit the church and walk in the former gardens.

'Stunning' is the only word to describe the church. The plain exterior does not prepare you for the magnificence inside. Amid a riot of gilt moulding 23 paintings decorate the ceiling, while 10 windows by the same Venetian artist add further colour. A balustraded gallery at the west end contains a very elegant organ, and the pulpit and lectern, though Victorian, match the rest of the exuberant decor. The dominant feature, however, is the huge monument to the first Lord Foley, a splendidly ostentatious piece of work. It is rather deflating to learn that this magnificent Baroque interior was not lovingly created by the *nouveau riche* landowner; the ceiling paintings, windows and various other fittings were bought as a job lot when the Duke of Chandos sold his Edgware mansion in 1735. The church is certainly a credit to its restorers. It may soon be possible to walk among the ruins of the house itself, but in the meantime some idea of the scale of things can be gained by inspecting the fountains in the garden, both of them of gigantic proportions.

The A443 continues east and reaches the Severn at Holt. Holt actually consists of three settlements. The old village is downstream from the bridge and well off the main roads, while Holt Heath is a modern development on the A4133. Holt Fleet is a curious collection of dwellings, some permanent, some distinctly temporary and ramshackle, clustered round the bridge (yet another by Telford). It grew up in a random sort of way to cater for river pursuits — fishing, sailing and boating — on this very attractive stretch of the Severn. It is a good place for a riverside walk, altough it is difficult to leave the car without patronising the pub.

Rather than take the direct road to Worcester from here, cross the bridge and travel the two miles or so to

Ombersley. Before it was bypassed, this attractive village used to be strangled by traffic, but now it is a pleasant experience to walk along the tranquil village street and look at some fine old houses. Several are timber-framed (the King's Arms is particularly impressive) but the brick cottages, especially the row opposite the church gate, contribute a good deal to the village's unpretentious charm.

Ombersley is the domain of the Sandys family of nearby Ombersley Court, and their memorials are contained in a preserved section of the old church adjacent to the present St Andrews, which looks richly medieval but is in fact an early example of nineteenth-century Gothic by Thomas Rickman. Like much of Rickman's work it has some fanciful features — the chancel, for example, is flanked by arches of almost Oriental character embellished with icing-sugar decoration. A rather endearing curiosity is the old heating stove in the north aisle, scrupulously constructed in authentic Gothic style. To the social historian the seating arrangements will be of interest, since they range from the substantial squire's pew through the solidly respectable family boxes to the painful-looking 'free seats' at the back.

The final approach to Worcester entails a return to the A443. 3 miles south of Holt Heath is Thorngrove House, home for a time of Lucien Bonaparte, Napoleon's brother, who was forced into exile for marrying an unsuitable wife. Almost immediately after come the first signs of Worcester's suburban sprawl, which has virtually destroyed the village character of Hallow. The big Victorian church is worth a visit, but before you reach it there is a chance to take the Lower Broadheath road to Elgar's birthplace. The right turn is signposted in the middle of Hallow.

The small cottage, close to the river Teme and facing the Malvern Hills, houses a large collection of scores and memorabilia relating to the life and work of the composer, and visitors have no difficulty in understanding why Elgar never lost his sense of belonging to this part of Worcestershire.

From here the city is entered on the west side of the river, and it is advisable to cross the bridge and seek out one of the riverside car parks rather than get involved in Worcester's complex traffic system.

The other route from Stourport to Worcester involves leaving Stourport on the B4193, and the first feature of interest, Hartlebury Castle, comes after about 3 miles. Bishops of Worcester have lived here since the thirteenth century, although the original castle was virtually gutted during the Civil War. The present building is a dignified country house of predominantly eighteenth-century Gothic appearance and the Bishop occupies only part of it, the remainder being given over to the County Museum. Both parts are open to the public, though at different times. The outstanding rooms of the Bishop's residence are the Great Hall, the Library and the Saloon, while the museum covers a vast range of interests relating to Worcestershire life and work.

The road now joins the A449 and it is necessary to turn left towards Kidderminster and then right on to the A450 after a mile. Follow this road to its junction with the A448 and turn towards Bromsgrove. Very soon you pass Harvington Hall and 3 miles later Chaddesley Corbett lies just off the road. This is a most attractive village with a main street of picture-postcard quality. The timber-framed Talbot Inn catches the eye, but the whole village deserves a leisurely walk. The church has a unique dedication to St Cassian and possesses a fine chancel and east window, but is noted mainly for a carved twelfth-century font.

The next destination is Droitwich, and it is best to avoid entering Bromsgrove by taking the minor road through Brockencole and Elmbridge; the connoisseur of churches, however, may want to continue on the main road as far as Dodford, where the Edwardian church is a fascinating example of 'arts and crafts' Gothic: an Art Nouveau style with decorations by the Bromsgrove Guild of craftsmen. The structure of the building, with its cloisters and outdoor

Ombersley

pulpit, is unusual and its rose window is famous. The village, too, is of some interest since it was first laid out in 1848 as one of the Chartist 'national Land Scheme' projects.

Droitwich makes no claim to beauty but has an unusually interesting history. The Romans had a small settlement here producing salt, and it was the salt of the Salwarpe valley that gave the town its medieval status; it gained a borough charter as early as the twelfth century. Salt is extracted from brine, and the early method of production was to use the brine that sprang naturally from the ground, but in the early eighteenth century pumps were introduced to force up purer and more concentrated brine. This led to the formation of subterranean caverns which have been a cause of subsidence ever since in the old part of the town.

It was no accident that as salt-production diminished, Droitwich found new prosperity as a spa. During the spa craze people needed very little

convincing that bathing in brine was beneficial, and in 1836 the Royal Baths were opened. Until recently modern treatment rooms were in operation, relying not so much on the curative powers of the brine but on its ability to support patients who could benefit from exercise in water. Now Droitwich's period as a spa has come to an end, but it has once again been offered a new lease of life as an overspill town with light industry.

The result is a rather featureless sprawl with the old town preserved at its centre like a museum piece. The High Street has a curiosity value with so many of its shops leaning at drunken angles because of subsidence (the freezer shop in the middle is spectacularly awry) but the general effect is shabby. At the southern end of the street the old Town Hall retains its black and white elegance, with pilasters, cornices and striking windows, and in Friar Street beyond there are some pleasant Georgian houses also sagging in unexpected places. The

Main Street, Ombersley

recently-restored Priory House graces the far end of Friar Street, although its effect is diminished by its position beneath an embankment carrying a new road.

St Andrew's Street, leading uphill from the Town Hall, contains the rambling length of the Raven Hotel, an odd mixture of genuine and reproduction timber-framing. It looks on to the newly-developed Victoria Square with its modern shopping parades, one of which is in a remarkable mock-Tudor style. Close by, in Heritage Way, is the Droitwich Heritage Centre, with displays illustrating the history and development of the town.

In 1197 Richard Wych was born in Droitwich. He entered the church and made rapid progress, becoming Chancellor of Oxford University and Bishop of Chichester. After his death he was canonised as St Richard of Chichester and is commemorated in an astonishing mosaic in the Roman Catholic church in Worcester Road. The town's two medieval parish churches, St Andrew's and St Peter's, are also worth visiting, but can boast nothing as striking.

The most impressive building here is about half a mile to the north off the A38. The dominant figure in the more recent history of Droitwich was John Corbett, the nineteenth-century industrialist who centralised salt production at Stoke Prior to the north-east of the town and played a major part in the development of the spa. In 1869 he commissioned a French architect to build him a mansion near the town (he allegedly wanted to give his French wife something to remind her of home). The result was a huge and highly-embellished house in the style of a Loire chateau; in fact it has always been known as Chateau Impney. Since it is now a hotel it is possible to sneak in and take a look at this eccentric masterpiece.

From Droitwich the main road to Worcester passes through Martin Hussingtree, which has some

PLACES OF INTEREST IN AND AROUND DROITWICH

Heritage Centre
Heritage Way. Local history, especially of salt industry and spa. Also temporary exhibitions.

Church of the Sacred Heart
Worcester Road. Superb mosaic decorations commemorating St Richard of Chichester.

Avoncroft Museum of Buildings
Stoke Heath, $4\frac{1}{2}$ miles north-east of Droitwich. Unique collection of restored and re-erected buildings, including windmill, granary, chain-making workshop, timber-framed houses, post-war prefabricated buildings.

Hanbury Hall
4 miles east of Droitwich. House of 1701, with fine furniture and porcelain. Outstanding feature is series of painted ceilings.

Jinny Ring Craft Centre
At Hanbury, 4 miles east of Droitwich. Weaving, pottery, glass, wood-carving etc.

Clacks Farm
Boreley, $4\frac{1}{2}$ miles west of Droitwich off A449. Garden featured in BBC television programme *Gardener's World*.

Chateau Impney
1 mile north of Droitwich off A38. Flamboyant nineteenth-century hotel, originally mansion built French chateau style.

picturesque buildings including the handsome eighteenth-century rectory and Court Farm of a century earlier. The churchyard is the resting place of Thomas Tomkins, organist at Worcester cathedral for 53 years, whose status as a composer might have been greater if he had not been forced into retirement by the Puritan regime. He lived at Court

*Danzey Green Windmill,
re-erected at the
Avoncroft Museum of
Buildings*

*Severn Valley Railway,
Hampton Loade Station*

Farm during the last years of his life.

If you are not familiar with Worcester, which has a reputation for being hostile to strange motorists, it is advisable to follow the A38 into the city and turn right just before the centre to park by the riverside.

3 Worcester and the Malverns

The development of Worcester has been the subject of heated debate ever since the 1950s, when plans were first put forward for the reshaping of the city centre. At that time it was a very picturesque place. It had a long waterfront of residential and commercial buildings to the north and south of the bridge. The area around the cathedral, and at the back of the main street, abounded in old cottages and shops threaded by narrow lanes.

During the 1960s a massive clearance took place, and the difference will be obvious to the visitor. For years a major problem was the traffic congestion caused by the solitary bridge, and this has led to new roads being given disproportionate priority within the city. A second bridge has now been constructed to the south, but it is well outside the city boundary and seems to have done little to alleviate the problem except at peak commuter periods.

In recent years much has been done to improve the river frontage to the north of the bridge, but to the south the cathedral dominates a very undistinguished riverside scene. The area in front of the cathedral consists mainly of a large roundabout and associated roads, and not much remains of Worcester's medieval heritage.

All this is mentioned, not to revive old controversies, but to warn the visitor not to expect too much. Worcester has never in any case been a mellow, leisurely, ecclesiastical city, but instead a busy commercial centre that happened to have a cathedral. In modern times its predominant character has been Georgian and Victorian, with thriving industrial activity that produced slum quarters which were anything but picturesque. This in itself justifies much

of the redevelopment, but in the process a good deal that could have contributed to an attractive townscape has been lost.

Luckily, enough individual features remain to make a tour of the city rewarding, and the best place to start is on the bridge. The Severn is impressively wide here, and the sight of the old warehouses to the south is a reminder of the part the river has played in Worcester's history. For centuries there was a thriving trade with the port of Bristol, and the city's main importance as an inland port was enhanced with the arrival of the Worcester and Birmingham Canal in 1815. The main dock area was at Diglis, but old photographs show the quayside between the cathedral and the bridge lined with small commercial craft.

As you walk into the city by way of Bridge Street the first building is a block of flats imaginatively designed to echo the old warehouse architecture, but Bridge Street itself bears all the signs of decay, not surprisingly since it is cut off from the main shopping streets by a complicated road junction. Bearing right into Deansway, the first of Worcester's notable churches is reached. Built on a high bank, All Saints' was started in 1739 and has the restrained classicism characteristic of the period. At the time of writing its future is uncertain, and it may be difficult to go inside, but the interior retains Georgian harmony in spite of Victorian restoration. In the south aisle there is a notable memorial to Samuel Matthew, a local merchant. Further up Deansway, past All Saints', it is worth crossing the road and going up the narrow lane leading into a group of older buildings. Tucked away here is the Countess of Huntingdon's Church, which has been under threat for years. It

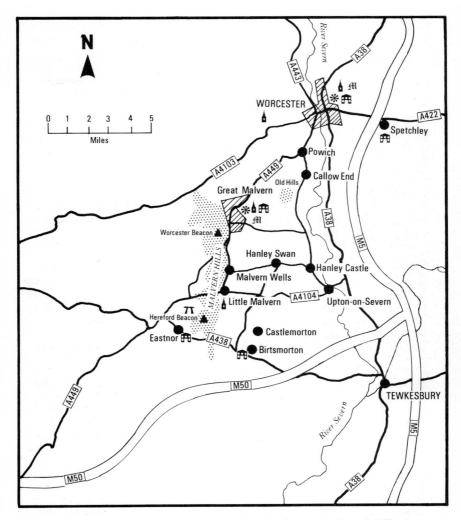

Map labels:
- N
- 0 1 2 3 4 5 Miles
- River Severn
- A443
- A38
- WORCESTER
- M
- A422
- Spetchley
- A4103
- Powich
- A449
- Callow End
- Great Malvern
- Old Hills
- M
- Worcester Beacon
- A38
- M5
- MALVERN HILLS
- Hanley Swan
- Hanley Castle
- Malvern Wells
- Little Malvern
- A4104
- Upton-on-Severn
- Hereford Beacon
- Eastnor
- A438
- Castlemorton
- Birtsmorton
- M50
- A449
- M50
- River Severn
- TEWKESBURY
- M5
- A38

was built in 1804, though the Countess first visited Worcester to establish her nonconformist sect in 1769. Again it may be difficult to gain access, but those who persist will find one of John Betjeman's favourite interiors.

Back in Deansway, a varied architectural scene confronts the onlooker. On the left is the police station in respectable 'civic Georgian'. On the right is the squat, khaki technical college with a notorious stretch of wasteland stretching down behind it to the river.

Overshadowing it all, and difficult to appreciate from here, is the soaring 'Glover's Needle', a superbly graceful 150ft spire. It is all that is left of St Andrew's church but is worthily retained as an asset to an otherwise nondescript skyline. At the top of Deansway on the right is the Old Palace, a mid-eighteenth-century house that was the Bishop's town residence until about 1840, when it was decided that he could manage with Hartlebury Castle. It was then used as the Deanery but today

The Severn at Worcester

serves as a diocesan centre. Actually the Georgian façade conceals earlier building of various dates, including a fourteenth-century basement known as the 'Abbot's Kitchen'.

The north side of the cathedral now comes fully into view and so does the most dramatic result of redevelopment. As you face the roundabout, with your back to Deansway, the pedestrianised High Street leads away to the left; the massive bulk of contemporary building in front is the Giffard Hotel with its associated shopping precinct. By way of contrast, some of the original character of this area can be seen around the corner to the right. This is Cathedral Yard, an oddly isolated survival comprising a handsome Georgian terrace with a raised pavement, hinting at what was once a quietly elegant cathedral close.

Access to the cathedral is across the green and through the north door. Although there were monastic foundations here well before the Normans, the earliest parts of the present building date from the reconstruction begun in 1084 by Bishop Wulfstan, the only Saxon bishop allowed to keep his diocese. After collapse in 1175 and a fire soon afterwards a long period of rebuilding began in 1218, and there was extensive restoration in the 1870s.

Detailed guides are available and only the more distinctive features of the cathedral can be mentioned here. The extreme west end is the oldest part of the nave (mid-twelfth century) although the large west window is by John Hardman and dates from the Victorian restoration. The nave was not finally completed until 1377. There are some fine tombs and monuments here, notably those of two former bishops — Thornborough and Hough — and the Worcester merchant Robert Wilde. More recent memorials include those to Stanley Baldwin, the novelist Francis Brett Young and Mrs Henry Wood, a Worcester lady famous as the author of 'East Lynne'.

The choir is a most graceful structure with octagonal columns of sandstone and marble and a general effect of lightness. In the centre is the tomb of King John who, at his own request, was the first post-Conquest king to be buried in England. The tomb thus has the oldest royal effigy in England, constructed in fine Purbeck marble. On the south side of the choir is the elaborate tomb of Prince Arthur, eldest son of Henry VII, who died in 1502. His chantry was built two years later and much of its splendour survives in spite of Puritan vandalism. The choir stalls have a set of misericords heavily restored in the nineteenth century.

Two of the original features of the cathedral should not be missed. The crypt is a magnificent Norman structure, while the Chapter House, reached from the south aisle, is unusual in being round with a central column. A passage leads from the Chapter House out into College Green, and there is a chance to walk down to the Watergate, an archway giving on to the river bank, to study the marks on the wall indicating the extraordinary levels the flooding Severn has reached in past years.

College Green was the site of Worcester Castle and is now a pleasant square lined with handsome buildings, most of them belonging to the King's School. At the far end the Edgar Tower forms an impressive entrance from the city; it dates from the reign of King John and was the castle gateway. Through the gateway on the left is a passage lined with mellow houses, mainly Georgian, while Severn Street leads away to the right. This is the way to one of the city's most popular tourist attractions, the Royal Worcester factory.

Worcester porcelain was the result of scientific experiments by John Wall, a local man of many parts who was a physician at the Royal Infirmary, a populariser of the Malvern waters and a dabbler in applied chemistry. It was in 1751 that he set up a company with the aim of copying the Chinese porcelain so popular at the time. The modern company is a direct descendant of Wall's enterprise and continues to produce celebrated collectors' pieces. The Dyson-Perrins museum at the works contains a superb collection of Worcester porcelain of all ages.

By continuing down Severn Street and turning left at the river bank, it is possible walk to Diglis basin, the terminus of the Worcester and Birmingham Canal. As at Stourport, the basins are occupied entirely by pleasure craft and there is little traffic these days at the big commercial wharves which can be seen further downstream. The canal towpath is a useful short cut to the

Commandery, the next stopping point (it is just beyond the second bridge). If you are returning directly from the porcelain works turn right at the end of Severn Street, cross Sidbury and walk the hundred yards to the bridge, where the unobtrusive Commandery entrance is signposted.

The Commandery got its name because it was the headquarters of the Royalist army at the battle of Worcester in 1651, but in fact the building is much older, having served as a monastic hospital and lodging house from about 1465. A programme of restoration has ensured the survival of the impressive timber-framed structure, and it is now a branch of the museum service, specialising, appropriately, in Civil War exhibits. Refreshments can be taken on the canalside terrace.

Walk back up Sidbury and cross the junction with the City Walls Road. Anyone interested in industrial archaeology would do well to walk a short distance along this road to look at the former Fownes Gloves factory — a massive nineteenth-century rectangular block, derelict but still standing at the time of writing. Otherwise take the next turning on the right into Friar Street, which looks unpromising because the planners sited a multi-storey car park at this end, but which in fact contains some of the city's oldest buildings.

Immediately on the left is the Old Talbot Inn, a hostelry that has had many uses in its time: it was originally an ecclesiastical house connected with the cathedral and later became the meeting place of the City Magistrates. Tudor House, a little further along on the same side, is another outpost of the City Museum and a very entertaining one. Dating from the fifteenth century, the house has also had a variety of uses as an inn, a shop, a tearoom and a clinic, but since 1971 it has housed the museum's 'folk' exhibits charting the history of everyday life in the area.

Almost immediately opposite are the Laslett Almshouses, built around an attractive quadrangle and looking comparatively modern. In fact they were erected in 1912 to replace some rather unsatisfactory accommodation in the old prison. Next door is Worcester's finest timber-framed building — the Greyfriars. Of late fifteenth-century date, it was probably the guest house of the friary and has been magnificently restored by private owners, although it now belongs to the National Trust. There is a most attractive garden behind.

Friar Street extends into New Street where there is also much of interest, although it has to be said that the street is long overdue for a facelift. To the left, the Market Hall has an interesting mid-Victorian frontage, while facing it is another fine timber-framed building, the three-storey Nash's House. John Nash helped to establish glove-making in the city in the sixteenth century, and among the benefactions of the family were the Nash and Wyatt Almshouses which, in their rebuilt form, can be seen by walking down Nash's Passage. Just beyond Nash's House is the melancholy sight of Worcester's first Wesleyan chapel. The plaque commemorating its inauguration by Wesley is still there, but the building itself looks almost derelict.

Finally, on the corner of New Street and the Cornmarket is another of Worcester's famous tourist attractions, King Charles's House. It has been restored to a suitably picturesque condition, although the two timber-framed sections are separated by a brick addition built after a fire in the eighteenth century. The house achieved fame after the battle of Worcester when Charles II, pursued by his Parliamentarian enemies, made his escape through the back door which opened on to the other side of the city wall.

The Cornmarket used to be an intimate square until demolition for the new City Walls Road opened up one side, but it is still a pleasant oasis with attractive shops and a fine Victorian pub on one corner. Easily overlooked at the

back of the pub is Old St Martin's church, externally undistinguished but with an interesting interior of the traditional Anglo-Catholic kind. Mealcheapen Street, one of the oldest in Worcester, leads out of the Cornmarket towards the city centre and passes through an ancient commercial district. Many of the buildings along here have been modernised — the opened-up courtyard of the Reindeer Inn is particularly successful — but it still retains more atmosphere than most of the neighbouring streets.

At the top is St Swithun's church, one of the best-preserved early eighteenth-century churches in Britain. Unfortunately, it is now redundant and its future is in doubt, but it is unthinkable that it will not be maintained in its present form, with its elegant proportions, restrained plasterwork, high box pews, gilded sanctuary columns and above all its splendid three-decker pulpit: the embodiment of a city church. The street behind it is the Trinity and contains Queen Elizabeth's House, so called because the Queen is reputed to have addressed the citizens from its balcony during her visit in 1575.

You now energe at the Cross, still the hub of Worcester although the traffic that used to dominate it has been diminished by the pedestrianisation of High Street. Turning right towards the railway bridge over the street, the buildings reflect better than anything else the city's past commercial prosperity. On the east side there is a very handsome range comprising two banks, St Nicholas' church and the old Hopmarket Hotel. The latter is an imposing Victorian structure, part of a complex that used to include warehouses and a market, and it has been imaginatively converted to accommodate small shops and craft establishments with flats above. Opposite is the Star, a former coaching inn much older than it looks.

The railway bridge marks the end of

Worcester Cathedral

the shopping centre but it is worth walking further along Foregate Street to reach another impressive Victorian building that houses the library, art gallery and main museum. Nineteenth-century work is a particular feature of the gallery's permanent collection, and there is usually a touring exhibition to see. The museum has some varied displays ranging from geology and natural history to a complete reconstruction of a traditional chemist's shop. The neo-classical Shire Hall of 1834 is set back from the road just beyond the museum, but the finest feature of Foregate Street is the long line of Georgian façades on the opposite side. The Odeon cinema strikes an incongruous note at one end, but its distinctive style will undoubtedly give it a place in the architectural history of Worcester in years to come.

Walk back along the west side of Foregate Street and note the inconspicuous entrance to the Berkeley Hospital on the other side of the railway bridge. The Berkeley family, whose ancestral home is Berkeley Castle near Bristol, has strong connections with Worcester. King Charles's House was their town residence and the family still occupies Spetchley Park on the eastern outskirts of the city. The present Hospital was built by Robert Berkeley in 1692 in a Dutch style, and it is charmingly situated around a flagged courtyard with a chapel at one end.

Almost opposite St Nicholas' church the narrow Angel Street makes an interesting diversion. At the point where it joins Angel Place there is the refurbished Corn Exchange of 1848, a solid, confident building with a colonnaded front. Next to it the old Scala is another and older example of classic cinema architecture. Angel Place runs into Broad Street, and a left turn brings you to the former Crown Inn, once Worcester's handsomest coaching inn and now converted into a shopping arcade.

Continue back to the Cross and turn

The Cathedral

Architecture ranging from eleventh to sixteenth centuries. Very fine crypt, tomb of King John, chantry of Prince Arthur, son of Henry VII.

City Museum and Art Gallery

Foregate Street
Archaeology, natural history, geology, military collections etc. Good permanent collection and touring exhibitions in Art Gallery.

The Commandery, Sidbury

Originally a fifteenth-century hospital with fine Great Hall. Houses museum of trades and industries and special display of Civil War items. Refreshments on canal bank.

Tudor House Museum, Friar Street

Very interesting museum of social life in city and county, with 'period' rooms.

Greyfriars, Friar Street

Superb fifteenth-century timber-framed house and garden.

Guildhall, High Street

Eighteenth-century building with celebrated decorative façade. Superb ballroom.

St Swithun's Church, The Cross

One of the best examples in Britain of an eighteenth-century city church.

Worcester Royal Porcelain Company, Severn Street

Factory tours, showroom, seconds shop. Also Dyson-Perrins Museum of Worcester Porcelain.

Berrow's Newspapers, Hylton Road

Tours demonstrating newspaper printing process.

Diglis Canal Basin, Riverside, half a mile south of Cathedral

Junction of Worcester and Birmingham Canal with river Severn.

Spetchley Park, 3 miles from city centre on A422.

House not open to public, but magnificent gardens with rare trees and deer park.

Elgar's Birthplace, Lower Broadheath

(route signposted from Hallow, $2\frac{1}{2}$ miles north of Worcester bridge on A443).
Cottage in which Elgar was born in 1857. Collection of scores, photographs, letters, personal mementoes etc.

Ravenshill Woodland Reserve, Alfrick, 6 miles west of Worcester off A4103.

Visitor Centre, trails, look-out tower.

Nunnery Wood Country Park, Off A442 on eastern outskirts of city.

Fifty-five acres of woodland being developed as country park.

right into the High Street. Apart from the shops there is nothing of great interest until the city's finest secular building, the Guildhall. This masterpiece of 1722 has a richly-embellished façade that includes statues of Charles I and Queen Anne and a caricature of Cromwell's head over the main door. The Guildhall is open to visitors and the great attraction is the assembly room on the first floor, with its beautifully-embossed and painted ceiling, its chandeliers and a small stage enhanced with delicate columns. This room was the scene of countless 'routs' — those provincial dances that were an essential part of the social life of the country gentry.

You are now back in the area that was comprehensively remodelled in the 1960s, but there are two reminders of former antiquity close by. A little way past the Guildhall is St Helen's church, a very old foundation indeed but heavily restored by the Victorians and now housing the county archives (it has the distinction of preserving the Bishop of Worcester's licence permitting William Shakespeare to marry Anne Hathaway). It stands on the corner of Fish Street where the timber-framed Farmer's Arms is a genuine reminder of old Worcester.

The way out of Worcester is across the bridge and through the undistinguished south-western suburbs on the A449. Just over a mile from the bridge there is a roundabout on the extreme edge of the city. Stay on the A449 but watch out for a lane on the right (signposted Lower Wick) a few hundred yards after. It leads to the old Powick bridge, a venerable structure of fifteenth-century origin and a scene of a very early skirmish in the Civil War. In September 1642 a consignment of valuable plate from various Oxford colleges was dispatched to Worcester as a contribution to the King's war funds. Pursuing Parliamentary forces made half-hearted attempt to enter the city but were repulsed, and having retired to Powick they were attacked by Royalist cavalry under Prince Rupert. After a bloody but indecisive engagement the Parliamentarians lost heart and retreated.

It was a different story in 1651 when Cromwell was triumphant in the decisive battle of the Civil War, fought mainly in the nearby fields on the far side of the new Powick bridge. The details of the battle are remembered only by the historians; what has passed into folklore is Charles's escape afterwards and his much-delayed voyage to France.

The lane over the bridge rejoins the main road close to an unexpected rural roundabout. The next village is Powick, a big and scattered settlement that has lost much of its character, although the church is worth visiting for a notable tomb of 1786 to a Mrs Russell by the artist Thomas Scheemakers. To find it turn left halfway round the island

created by a large house in the middle of the main road. (This same lane goes on to Callow End, a much-developed village noted as the site of Stanbrook Abbey. It is the home of an order of Benedictine nuns; it is a closed order so casual visitors are not encouraged, but the remarkable Victorian architecture of the Abbey, designed by E.W. Pugin in 1878, can be seen from the village street. The Old Hills on the other side of Callow End, are a fine stretch of undulating common, good for picnics and walking.)

The A449 continues towards Malvern, passing Powick Hospital on the left, where the young Elgar was conductor of the inmates' band. The hills loom ever nearer and the outskirts of Malvern are reached at Newland, a village where the splendid Victorian church is in a French Gothic style and stands near a set of almshouses provided by the Beauchamp family, whose principal home is Madresfield Court, a mile away.

There is ample evidence here and at Malvern Link of the common land that used to extend over a vast area beneath the hills. The nine-mile range rises sharply in an otherwise level landscape and presents a stark and distinctive silhouette. The hills look high but in fact they reach only 1400ft at their two highest points, and it is their accessibility that accounts for their popularity throughout the Midlands. Despite Victorian encroachment on the slopes at Great Malvern itself, the hills have remained free of intrusive development, thanks to the Malvern Hills Conservators, an old-established body with effective powers. There has been a certain amount of quarrying for the extremely hard pre-Cambrian rock, but the old workings are now well screened; indeed they are now something of an asset because they make visible the strata of the underlying stone. Moreover, a good deal of the charm of the town is due to the use of this local building material.

Some suggestions for exploring the

hills are included later in the chapter. Great Malvern, however, is the natural centre of the string of settlements along the hills. Leaving aside very early history, Malvern first acquired status as the site of a monastic foundation at the end of the eleventh century, although its situation well away from natural lines of communication discouraged the development of a town. At the Dissolution, Malvern was no more than a village, and it remained so until the turn of the eighteenth century, when the waters began to achieve fame for their curative properties. Dr John Wall (the moving spirit behind the Worcester Porcelain Company) first published an analysis of the waters as early as 1757. His novel claim was that their benefit derived from their purity and not from any mineral content, and this reputation still supports the thriving sale of bottled Malvern water.

Like many other towns, Malvern went on to prosper from the spa cult of the nineteenth century, although it never became the sort of fashionable resort that acquired a dubious reputation; indeed the hydropathic treatment at Malvern was not simply a matter of meeting to sip the waters but a spartan regime of cold douches and cold walks. This high-minded attitude is reflected in the architecture of the town, which has none of the expensive elegance of Bath or Cheltenham, and certainly no frivolity. Instead there is a preponderance of solid Victorian villas, although it must be said that some of them show individual and sometimes adventurous taste, and their general effect has been to create a leafy spaciousness in the roads near the town centre.

The best place to start a walk round the town is in Belle Vue Terrace, a short length of the A449 that cuts across the top of Malvern and forms its highest shopping street. The Terrace lives up to its name because from here the Priory and the other major buildings can be seen against a backdrop of much of the county of Worcestershire. At the height of the water-cure period this was the centre of activity. The Mount Pleasant hotel at the southern end is the only surviving hotel of the time, while Lloyd's Bank next door stands on the site of the first hydropathic centre of 1842. Next door again the shop was once the Belle Vue hotel, and the building still retains much of its original appearance. Further along there are two other shops of interest; the impressive Pharmacy fulfilled this function for visitors in town for the cure, and W.H. Smith's was Malvern's Post Office in stagecoach days.

Just around the corner of the northern end of the Terrace is the Unicorn Inn, self-consciously quaint now, but with genuine timber-framing and one of Malvern's oldest survivals. Another interesting group stands on the opposite side of the road. Barclay's Bank is in the best Grecian style of the Regency period and was erected to house the Royal Library, with the 'Coburg Baths' incorporated into the other section of the building. These two establishments formed an important social centre, since the Library offered a range of cultural activities to complement the serious business of medical treatment. Equally typical of its period, the adjacent Foley Arms is a handsome coaching inn of 1810.

Immediately below Belle Vue Terrace is the open space that was once the 'village green' of medieval Malvern; the old parish church stood on the site now occupied by the post office. Walk over to the south side and down the road leading to the Abbey Gateway, noting on the left the shop built in a well-meaning 'Gothic' style. The Gateway spans the road and looks impressively medieval, but its nineteenth-century reconstruction left little of the original work visible. The nearby Abbey Hotel looks much more venerable but dates from 1849. The backs of houses are always instructive, and a glance at the huge Victorian house up on the right

reveals some remarkable architectural details in the timbering and windows.

Continue down Abbey Road and turn left into Grange Road, passing the site of the original priory, now covered by hotel buildings. On the right is the pleasant Priory Park and then the Winter Gardens. The first buildings here were the Assembly Rooms, essential for a spa but appearing rather belatedly in 1884; in the 1920s the present building was erected to house a theatre and other amenities, and up to the second world war it was the venue of the famous Malvern Festival where several of Shaw's plays received their first performances.

A path immediately opposite the Winter Gardens leads round to the main door of the Priory, one of England's outstanding parish churches. It has had

a chequered history. Begun in the eleventh century and still basically Norman, its present form is largely the result of extensive rebuilding between 1400 and 1460, yet only 79 years after this complete renewal it was surrendered to Henry VIII at the Dissolution. The other Priory buildings were very quickly disposed of to opportunist buyers and a start was made on demolishing the church. Then, at the last moment, the inhabitants of the tiny village offered to buy it from the King to replace their old church. They got it for £20, but the maintenance of the huge building was another matter; it proved such a burden that by the beginning of the nineteenth century the church was in a serious state of disrepair and hardly usable. Not until 1860 was radical restoration put in hand, so it is surprising that so much survives

The Priory
Norman origin but mainly the result of fifteenth-century rebuilding. Splendid interior, with fifteenth-century glass, misericords and outstanding collection of medieval tiles.

Museum, Abbey Gateway.
Mainly local history.

Winter Gardens and Priory Park,
Grange Road.
Theatre and other entertainments, very attractive gardens.

St Anne's Well
Traditional source of Malvern water; interesting nineteenth-century building.

Worcestershire Beacon
Highest point of Malvern Hills with superb views. Accessible from many points, including St Anne's Well.

Herefordshire Beacon
Spectacular Iron Age fort, accessible from car park at Wynds Point near Little Malvern.

Little Malvern Priory, on A4104, 4 miles south of Great Malvern.
Interesting priory church with adjacent remains of monastic buildings in Little Malvern Court.

St Wulfstan's Roman Catholic Church
on A449 south of Malvern Wells.
Grave of Sir Edward Elgar and his wife in churchyard.

Newland Church and Almshouses On A449, 3 miles north of Great Malvern.
Interesting group of nineteenth-century almshouses with church of same period in French style.

Birtsmorton Waterfowl Sanctuary
Birtsmorton, 8 miles south of Great Malvern off A38.
A seven acre natural reserve housing over eighty species.

Eastnor Castle On A438, 2 miles west of Malvern Hills.
Castle built in 1814. Pictures, furniture, armour, tapestries etc. Fine grounds with large lake.

Old Hills Callow End, $2\frac{1}{2}$ miles south of Powick on A449 between Malvern and Worcester.
Extensive area of open common land, good walking.

in a building of immense beauty.

There is an immediate impression of space upon entering because nothing impedes the view of the entire length of nave and chancel. As so often with Victorian restoration most attention was given to the east end, so there is a marked contrast between the solid strength of the nave and the lighter richness of the chancel. The nave arcades of six bays are supported by massive pillars, and some of the fifteenth-century granite can be seen towards the top. Although the tower divides the east and west ends there is very little sense of its presence thanks to the lofty arches beneath it.

The interior features of the Priory are described in great detail in a booklet illustrated in colour and available at the bookstall. There is a notable array of fifteenth-century glass, not only in the east window but in the clerestory, the north transept and the west window, while good Victorian glass can be seen in St Anne's Chapel (south choir aisle). The misericords are all in place in the monks' stalls in the choir, although the originals are mixed with nineteenth-century restorations or replicas — the carvings include ten of the twelve 'Labours of the Months'. The Priory's

Winter on the Malverns

most famous passession, however, is a collection of well over a thousand medieval tiles, locally made. Some are incorporated into the altar screen but most are to be found in the north choir aisle. It is perhaps worth pointing out the ironic fact that the most elaborate tomb here, between the choir and St Anne's Chapel, commemmorates John Knotsford, the Elizabethan entrepreneur mainly responsible for demolishing most of the other monastic buildings.

After leaving the Priory you can continue the tour of the town centre by walking back to the Winter Gardens and strolling through Priory Park. The gardens are small but cleverly landscaped and include several varieties of exotic trees and the Swan Pool, originally the monks' fish pond. Two very contrasting buildings can be seen by leaving at the north gate; Priory Park mansion is a remarkable example of unrestrained Victorian Gothic, while Portland House (on the opposite side of Church Street) is in severe classical style.

Malvern's real character is to be found by walking along some of the spacious roads lined with Victorian architecture in infinite variety. Highly recommended are Graham Road, which runs north from Church Street, and Avenue Road. The latter branches off almost opposite Portland House and leads to the interesting railway station, but for the architectural enthusiast the main attraction will probably be the huge façade of the Girls' College, designed by E.W. Elmslie as the Imperial Hotel in 1861.

Victorian building development was strongly influenced by Viscountess Foley, who adopted the role of Lady of the Manor and imposed much of her own distinctive taste on the town (among other decrees she is reputed to have stipulated that none of the larger houses built in her time should be similar). Among her other achievements was the embellishment of St Anne's Well, one of Malvern's natural springs. It can be visited by returning to Belle Vue Terrace and taking the lane that starts at the Unicorn Inn. The Well is one point on a circular walk around the lower contours of the hills on a well-defined path that passes through Rushy Valley to the south and goes on to provide a fine view of the town, including the famous Malvern College. Soon after passing Earnslaw quarry and pool, and just short of the Wyche cutting, the track turns on to the other side of the ridge and proceeds northwards, taking in the former site of the Royal Well Spa and the indicator

stone on the north side of the Worcestershire Beacon. From here there is a zigzag progress back to St Anne's Well.

Innumerable other walks are possible from the car parks sited close to the top of the ridge. Ideal starting points are the 'cuttings' — the Wyche, Wynd's Point and Hollybush — where roads cross the hills. The most popular expedition is to the top of the Herefordshire Beacon, reached by a path starting at the Wynd's Point car park, but equally worthwhile (and rather less patronised) are the ridge walks possible from the car parks on the B4232 at 150:766422 and 150:766450.

Enthusiastic ramblers may well want to spend a day on the complete ridgetop walk, although this requires the organisation of private transport to reach or leave the southern end. It makes sense to start at the northern end where the climbing is steeper, and there is a path up to North Hill beginning at 150:770470. It is a steep ascent between disused quarries. Once on the top there

The Malvern Hills

The British Camp, Malvern Hills

are two summits visible ahead; purists will no doubt want to walk over the Sugar Loaf before tackling the Worcestershire Beacon, but others may prefer to take the comfortable track around to the right.

Various paths lead to the top of the Beacon, which is so popular that a cafe operates on a seasonal basis (but do not rely on finding it open). A toposcope helps to identify the features of the view from the top; some of the markings are a little optimistic but it is a splendid panorama, and the sense of height is such that it is easy to forget that you are standing at only 1400ft. A well-defined path leads off and down directly to the Wyche Cutting, where the B4218 crosses the hills.

The next length of ridge is pleasantly undulating and the path starts to run close to the Shire Ditch, a thirteenth-century boundary created by the Earl of Gloucester and the Bishop of Hereford to mark the division between their

hunting grounds. Later it was part of the county boundary between Worcestershire and Herefordshire. Wynd's Point, the end of this section, is a very popular spot for visitors seeking a short route to the Herefordshire Beacon, and it is also a convenient place for a refreshment break.

At 1100ft the Beacon is another magnificent viewpoint, this time towards the rougher, less inhabited country to the west of the hills. It is also the site of an Iron Age hill fort with some spectacular ramparts and ditches. Comparatively few people venture further south, but this section, through a broken and wooded landscape, makes a pleasant change from the exposed ridge to the north.

The path continues to follow the Shire Ditch below Hangman's Hill, passing an outcrop containing the mysteriously-named Clutter's Cave. The obelisk over on the right is in the grounds of Eastnor Castle and commemmorates members of the Somers family. Several tracks meet at the point known as Silurian Pass (to mark an underlying bank of younger Silurian stone) and the way lies over or round the modest Swinyard Hill. The dangerous Gullet Quarry lies straight ahead and it is best to skirt it on the right before making for Midsummer Hill (930ft). A track that skirts the hill on the right avoids the climb; otherwise you need to branch east at 150:758387 and pass through the 'north gates' of the Iron Age ramparts. Inside the ramparts there are paths leading to Midsummer Hill or to Hollybush Hill, its neighbour to the east.

In fact the route by way of Hollybush Hill is possibly the more interesting, if longer, because the descent is through the 'south gates' of the fort, which have been extensively excavated, and then through the old Hollybush quarry, a source of valuable roadstone until fairly recently. Either path leads to the hamlet of Hollybush.

Unless it is a point of honour to scale every summit there is little to be gained from climbing Raggedstone Hill to the south of Hollybush; the recommended route is east along the A438 for 300yd and then into the lane on the right opposite the entrance to the quarry. Keep to the left when the path branches and follow a contour with the hill on the right. The way lies through woodland and emerges at the romantically-named and picturesque hamlet of White-leaved Oak. Chase End Hill, the southernmost summit of the range, lies a short distance away. It is a fairly steep climb to an unfrequented spot, but worth it for the sense of achievement at the end of an exhilarating ten mile walk.

Looking down from the hills at the open countryside stretching across the Severn it is difficult to believe that the area was once thick forest, part of the 7000 acres of woodland that surrounded the Malvern range. From the time of William the Conqueror onwards it was under direct royal jurisdiction with its own officers and laws. When the Earl of Gloucester married the daughter of Edward I, the forest was made over to him and became Malvern Chase. During the next 200 years large areas of the forest were cleared, parts were colonised, and by the time of Charles I a large number of people had claimed squatters' rights. In 1632 the position was regularised by royal decree; the king kept one third and the remainder was made available to the dwellers as 'commoners'.

There is little woodland left now but the area still has the unmistakable air of commonland, with long straight roads linking the hills and the river. Something of the atmosphere of the Chase can be appreciated in the course of a drive from Great Malvern, across the hills and round the southern end to Upton-on-Severn.

From the centre of Great Malvern take the A449 south through Malvern Wells. After passing through watch out for a minor road descending steeply to the left and signposted Upton; almost immediately after it you can turn into the drive of St Wulfstan's Roman Catholic Church, where Edward Elgar and his wife are buried in the churchyard. The A4104 now branches to the left, and a short distance along it is Little Malvern Priory, set back from the road on the right. It is a strange-looking building — the surviving tower and chancel of the former priory church. At the Dissolution the monastic buildings passed into private ownership (the adjacent Little Malvern Court incorporates some of them) but the usable parts of the church were made over to the parishioners. It has retained some of its medieval glass, the misericord stalls, unfortunately without most of their carving, and some tiles similar to those in Malvern Priory.

Return from here to the A449 which climbs up to Wynd's Point. From here the road descends into the Herefordshire countryside, and there is a rather dull stretch before a left turn on to the A438 and Eastnor. The main attraction here is the early nineteenth-century castle set beside a lake, but the village itself is attractive with thatched cottages and a green. The church interior is very dark but notable for an ornate marble and gilt reredos and the alabaster memorial to the second Earl Somers.

After Eastnor the road crosses the hills again almost imperceptibly at Hollybush and emerges on to Malvern Chase. Birtsmorton Court lies up a minor road on the left about four miles later; it is semi-fortified with a moat and has many historical associations, including the fact that Cardinal Wolsey was family chaplain there as a young man. Much later William Huskisson, the early nineteenth-century politician, was born there. The Court is not open to the public but the exterior can be seen from the adjacent churchyard. There are some fine memorials in the church, among them a huge altar tomb lacking its effigy and an unusual wall monument to Admiral William Caldwell, showing his ship and an interesting collection of navigational intruments. The stained glass in the north chancel wall shows the murder of Thomas à Becket, to whom the church was dedicated before the Reformation.

After visiting Birtsmorton it is worth retracing the route for just a over a mile and taking the B4208 to Welland. The road crosses Castlemorton Common, a stretch of unenclosed country largely unaffected by modern development. Go straight through Welland and after a mile turn right on to the minor road to Hanley Swan. The most interesting building here is not in the village itself but a mile to the north — the Roman Catholic church, which has a most sumptuous interior dating from 1846, the result of benefactions from the Hornyold family of nearby Blackmore Park.

Return to the crossroads at Hanley Swan, turn left on to the B4209 and right at the junction with the B4211. After half a mile the village of Hanley Castle lies just off the road to the right. It is rather genteel but undeniably attractive, with a tiny green and an intimate group of houses. There is not much sign of the castle now but parts of the medieval church survive, supplemented by a tower, chancel and north chapel built of brick in the seventeenth century. It contains some good monuments to the Lechmeres, the local family associated with the village for centuries; most are in the chapel but there is one very distinguished memorial in the nave. The Victorian glass is unusually vivid, the reds and blues of the west window being almost flamboyant.

Outside, apart from the elaborately-restored houses, is a picturesque pub called the Three Kings and, unexpectedly, a large secondary school. It was established by the Lechmeres as early as 1544, and as its varied buildings show it has been steadily enlarged since. Having served as a state grammar school for boys it has now become comprehensive and co-educational, a remarkable example of continuity and adaptation.

From here it is a short distance to Upton-on-Severn, and the main car park is on the right as you enter the town.

4 Upton-on-Severn to Gloucester

For many visitors, Upton will prove to be the most attractive of the Severnside towns. It has much in common with Bewdley both in geography and history; its period of greatest prosperity was in the eighteenth century when it rivalled Bewdley and Worcester as a river port, but unlike them it had little to fall back on when the river trade died. Consequently it became a modest country town and has retained much of its village atmosphere. In recent years pleasure craft have been attracted here, and there is an unobtrusive marina on the other side of the river.

Walk from the car park to the bridge. It is less than fifty years old, although one of its predecessors played an important part in the Civil War during the preliminaries to the battle of Worcester. The bridge was the only one between Worcester and Tewkesbury, and had been breached in order to deny it to the Parliamentary army, but someone had been careless enough to leave a plank lying across and the entire force of Ironsides was able to get over. The present bridge provides a good view of a miniature waterfront, where a walk round the town can begin.

At one time Upton was noted for its innumerable inns, and you pass two of them, the Plough and the King's Arms, before reaching a group of eighteenth-century warehouses that have been modernised but left with sufficient character to preserve the wharf atmosphere. There are always plenty of boats tied up along here, one of the permanent fixtures being a big river barge. By continuing along the riverside it is possible to see some of the interesting houses further downstream. The Malt House is probably the best — a very impressive Georgian mansion

with finely-detailed windows — but there is fine brickwork and unusual embellishment in an earlier building called the King's Stable just beyond. Severn House and Old Walls, both of the eighteenth century, complete the row.

Return towards the town but his time go along Dunn's Lane, which passes behind the warehouses. At the point where it branches off Waterside House is another fine Georgian structure, but the main attraction of Dunn's Lane is the group of cottages behind the Swan Inn. They are rather genteel now, and it is difficult to imagine this as a dirty and noisy alley as it was in the late eighteenth century, or in the 1830s when it was the centre of an outbreak of cholera.

Dunn's Lane leads into the High Street, with the timber-framed Anchor Inn on the corner; the large gable over the adjacent shop gives its date as 1601. The inn is the first in a line of harmonious old buildings on the left hand side of the High Street, including the elegant White Lion Hotel and the Talbot Head Hotel with its very distinctive windows. High Street extends into Old Street, though if you have time it is rewarding to turn left into Court Street and look at Court Row.

Old Street is narrow and its attractions are less obvious, but there is much to enjoy in the details of these unpretentious buildings that provide such a rich variety of façades. They are mainly Georgian and Victorian, though No 51 is an interesting timber-framed house of the seventeenth century, and tucked away behind wrought-iron gates just before it is a handsome Baptist chapel of 1734. At the end of Old Street the town suddenly comes to an end and the view is dominated by the lofty spire

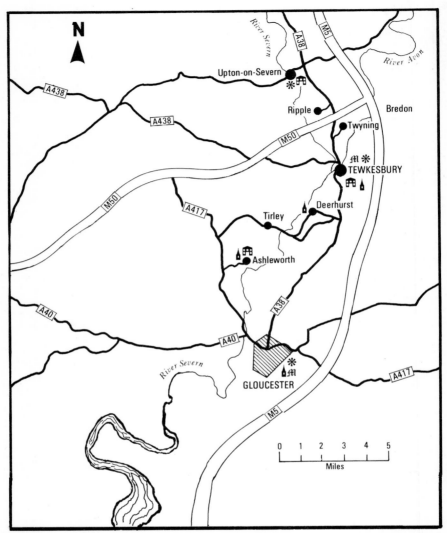

of the 'new' parish church, built in 1879
to replace the smaller one by the bridge.
Unfortunately its Bath stone has
obstinately refused to weather to a more
satisfactory colour than bilious yellow,
while the interior is solid and even
sumptuous without having any features
that could be called distinguished.

Return down Old Street and turn left
at the crossroads into New Street. There
are some rather over-prettified shops

with the date 1668 on the left, but once
again the attraction lies in the variegated
range of frontages on both sides. At the
bottom on the left is a plaque recording
the fact that the 'ducking pond' for
scolds was situated nearby.

As you return to the High Street and
walk towards the river the most
prominent feature ahead is Upton's
famous landmark, the Bell Tower. In
appearance it is a conventional church

Upton-on-Severn

Tewkesbury Abbey

Clockmakers' shop sign, Gloucester

Gloucester Dock

Talbot Head Hotel, Upton-on-Severn

tower with an incongruous cupola on the top, and the odd combination is explained by the fact that in 1754 a new nave and chancel were added to the fourteenth-century tower and the cupola was designed as a finishing touch to the church's new classical appearance. After the construction of the new and larger church the old one became redundant and the nave and chancel were removed in the 1930s. The Tower now houses the information centre and some informative displays of local history and geography.

The churchyard has been left as an open space with the old market cross looking down on the High Street at one end. There is a particularly interesting row of houses on the opposite side of Church Street, notably the well-restored Cromwell Cottages, late sixteenth-century and close-studded. Finally, on returning to the car park, note the attractive row of eighteenth-century cottages in the road leading to the bridge.

There are two easy riverside walks from Upton. The first follows the start of the town walk along the quay, but the lane by the river soon becomes a footpath that runs for two miles along the bank before turning at 150:856384 to join a track at Buryend Farm for the return to town.

The second begins on the other side of the bridge and follows the river for two miles northward, passing Severn End, the home of the Lechmere family, on the opposite bank. At point 150:842428 a path leads back to the bridge passing Ryall's Court.

The route now is into Gloucestershire and on to Tewkesbury by way of the A38, reached at a junction to the east of Upton. There is not much to stop for during the six mile run. Tewkesbury arrives very suddenly; there are no suburbs in this direction, and once across the Avon bridge you are in the middle of the town. The main car park is most easily reached by driving the length of the main street, turning left at the junction with the A438 and then watching for a sign a few hundred yards along on the left.

This, of course, is where the Avon finally joins the Severn, and medieval Tewkesbury was consequently a place of some importance. It had strong royal connections during its early history and was the scene of a major battle in 1471 during the Wars of the Roses. Economically it prospered on the wool trade and the busy commerce of the rivers. Nowadays the most obvious sign of its historic status is the Abbey, which still dominates the western end of the town and is the natural starting point for a walk.

Its sheer size and grandeur make it difficult to think of the Abbey in other than cathedral terms, although it is technically a parish church, purchased by the Corporation from Henry VIII at the Dissolution. Built by Robert Fitzhamon in the very early twelfth century with imported Caen stone, it has undergone several restorations since, but nothing has detracted from the basic simplicity of the cruciform exterior, graced with one of England's finest Norman towers.

Simplicity and strength are also the first impressions on entering the nave. The arcades are supported on huge round pillars and the vaulting above is functional rather than delicate. Since there is no intervening screen the contrast between the grey nave and the bright colour and light tracery of the choir roof is very striking. Almost all the interior embellishment has been concentrated at the east end, where there is a wealth of historical interest. Instead of the usual principal window, the east wall contains an arc of seven windows with magnificent fourteenth-century glass paid for by the widow of Hugh le Despenser. The Despensers and their complicated network of relatives had close associations with the Abbey, and they are commemorated by a famous group of chantries in the choir. Most date from the same period — the turn of the fourteenth century — and are encrusted with unbelievably elaborate filigree ornament.

At the back of the high altar a series of small chapels are ranged against the east wall, and among the interesting memorials is one grisly example portraying the partly-decomposed body of an abbot. Here too is a sixteenth-century 'Armada chest', designed to receive contributions towards the upkeep of the navy and fitted with an intricate lock that covers most of the lid. The older of the two organs dates from 1610. It was originally made for Magdalen College, Oxford, and was later presented to Oliver Cromwell, giving rise to a story that Milton played it at Hampton Court.

A tour of the town from the Abbey gates should start with a walk down Mill Street, directly opposite. There are two notable buildings at the bottom by the river. The nineteenth-century mill (now a restaurant) formed part of the setting of Mrs Craik's 'John Halifax, Gentleman', a novel with many other local associations. Close by is the attractive rough-hewn granary, originally part of the Abbey buildings and now restored. Back at the top of Mill Street, the Bell Hotel of about 1696 accommodated Mrs Craik while she was writing her novel, but rather more pleasing to the eye jaded by so much timber-framing is the simple and elegant National School of 1813 that stands nearby.

The centre of Tewkesbury is Y-shaped, which makes a circular tour difficult, but most of the interesting buildings lie in Church Street and High Street which run parallel to the old course of the Avon. Running behind the frontages are a number of alleyways that once teemed with squalid life but now provide quiet oases away from the traffic. One of these is almost immediately on the left as you set off down Church Street. Old Baptist Chapel Court once contained a number of tiny medieval cottages, and in the 1620s three

Abbey Cottages, Tewkesbury

of them were combined into one of the earliest of England's nonconformist chapels. Recent work has restored the chapel to its original form, although some may find the odd yellow ochre paint rather jarring.

A unique survival can be seen on the other side of Church Street: the range of tiny fifteenth-century shops known as Abbey Cottages. They were basically primitive houses, transformed each day into shops by letting down the window shutters to form counters, and one of them has been left as a reconstruction. A Georgian house sits strangely in the middle of the row, but it is remarkable

that so many of the cottages survived. At the far end of them the John Moore Museum has been established to commemorate the well-known local novelist.

Interesting buildings come thick and fast as you walk towards the Cross. Most of them are timber-framed and of a kind that reflect urban prosperity rather than simple living. Craik House, the Old Hat Shop, Cross House, Warwick House and the Berkeley Arms all stand within a short distance of each other, while Lilley's Alley and Ancill's Court reveal the rewards of exploring behind the main street. All this antiquity

The House of the Nodding Gables, Tewkesbury

throws the Georgian façade of the Royal Hop Pole Hotel into greater prominence; apart from being extremely handsome (and older than it looks) it was the hotel chosen by Dickens for Mr Pickwick to lodge at.

At the Cross the forks of the Y branch off, with Church Street continuing to the left and becoming High Street. It is impossible to detail all the attractions along here. The guidebooks point with pride to obvious showpieces like the superb seven-bay Swan Hotel, the precariously-jettied 'House of the Nodding Gables', the Old Fleece, the Ancient Grudge restaurant and the Tudor House Hotel. They are certainly fine, but they distract attention from more modest buildings of great individuality.

The discerning visitor will want to look out for the late eighteenth-century Town Hall, which is surprisingly small, built of sandstone, decorated with pilasters and topped off with a cupola. Almost opposite is the Wheatsheaf restaurant, restrained in style and probably the most æsthetically pleasing timber-framed structure in the town.

Next to the Town Hall Lloyd's Bank occupies a spectacular piece of fakery that has genuine claims to distinction, while on the other side of the road Auriol House (1606) has a tall, slender frontage with a two-storey bow window. About 100 yards further up from Lloyd's is a most impressive Georgian mansion with a central entrance arch and Venetian windows above it on two floors.

At the far end of the High Street a left turn called Quay Street provides a vista of huge riverside buildings. On the right is the only uncompromisingly modern building in the town centre — the Roses Theatre, which achieved a sad niche in show-business history as the place where comedian Eric Morecambe collapsed and died after a performance. The Black Bear Inn, reputedly the oldest pub in Gloucestershire, marks the end of the street, and by turning left here you reach King John's bridge, first constructed in 1197 and much altered since.

Return now to the High Street, walk up Sun Street past the theatre and turn right into Oldbury Road, where you pass Holy Trinity Church. This is another building not mentioned in the guidebooks, but its rather ordinary brick façade conceals a most elegant early nineteenth-century church, characteristically spacious and uncluttered. It is the only Anglican church apart from the Abbey, and in its heyday it was obviously the place of worship preferred by the humbler section of the population; to accommodate them it was necessary to have two tiers of galleries. Follow Oldbury Road to its end and you emerge into Tewkesbury's third main thoroughfare, Barton Street.

The architecture here is on a smaller scale and more humdrum in character; mainly Georgian and Victorian but none the worse for that. A notable pair of half-timbered houses have been converted to form a museum and information centre. Further back towards the Cross on the left is a former Baptist church that looks as if it might once have been a small coaching inn. It faces a line of small shops with faded but interesting early Victorian frontages. The tour is completed by walking back along Church Street to the Abbey.

The M5 or A38 will take you quickly on to Gloucester but a less direct and more leisurely route gives an opportunity to visit two places of particular interest on the way.

Leave Tewkesbury on the A38 and after three miles turn right on to the B4213. After another half-mile a minor road branches off to Deerhurst. The village itself is not especially remarkable but it was of some importance in Saxon times; King Edmund and King Canute met here in 1016 to sign a treaty redrawing the boundary between Saxons and Danes. The reason for its pre-eminence was its priory, probably founded in the seventh century and destined to become the leading religious foundation of the kingdom of Hwicce. Its influence declined with the foundation of abbeys at Tewkesbury and Gloucester, and at the Dissolution it was sold to the Throckmorton family.

PLACES OF INTEREST IN AND AROUND TEWKESBURY

The Abbey
One of Britain's finest Norman towers. Splendid interior containing fourteenth-century glass, notable chantry tombs, seventeenth-century organ.

Tewkesbury Museum Barton Street
Displays illustrating history of town.

John Moore Museum Church Street
Commemorates novelist who set his stories in the Tewkesbury area. Natural history, domestic bygones, farming.

The Little Museum Church Street
One of a line of unique cottage 'shops', furnished in domestic style of fifteenth century.

Old Baptist Chapel Off Church Street
Restored chapel that was originally a fifteenth-century house. First used by Baptists in 1623.

Deerhurst church 2 miles south of Tewkesbury off A38.
Thought to be the oldest church in England to which a date can be assigned. Interesting progression of architecture from Saxon times onwards. Unusual arrangement of pews round altar.

Odda's Chapel Near Deerhurst Church
Saxon chapel of 1056, discovered within farmhouse.

Midsummer Weavers London Lane, Upton-on-Severn, 6 miles north of Tewkesbury.
Workshop open to the public.

Its church, however, was converted for parish use, and thus it can claim to be among the very oldest churches in Britain (some say the oldest).

Characteristically herringbone masonry is visible on the outside and the interior shows evidence of several stages of building around the ancient nave that is the original core. But there are other interesting features apart from its architectural development. The richly carved Saxon font is the finest to be seen in this part of England. The memorial brass to Sir John Cassy and his wife (c1400) is one of only two in the country to show a pet dog with a name — Tirri. Eight pews have also survived from the fifteenth century, but perhaps the most striking evidence of continuity of worship here is the arrangement of pews around the altar for the celebration of Holy Communion in the puritan style.

Visible from the church gate and reached along a short lane is Odda's Chapel. It was discovered in 1885 within the framework of the house to which it is still attached, and a memorial stone dates it precisely at 1056. Barn-like in form, it consists of a surprisingly lofty nave and a small chancel in rough stone. Earl Odda was a friend of Edward the Confessor, and the Chapel was erected in memory of his brother.

The minor road out of Deerhurst to the south rejoins the B4213 near the point where it crosses the Severn over the lonely Haw Bridge and passes through Tirley, a pleasantly scruffy village. The countryside here is dotted with wooded hills and threaded with intricate, narrow lanes linking small hamlets; to avoid getting lost it is best to follow the road to its junction with the A417. A mile or so later you reach Hartpury where a left turn leads to Ashleworth.

This appears to be a conventional village, but if you turn down past the village green you arrive at the ancient riverside settlement. Very little remains of the once-important quay (flood banks have displaced it) and the ferry no longer runs. The former waterside inn now appears to be a private house. But three interesting buildings have survived close to the river. The tithe barn of about 1500 is like a smaller version of the better-known barns at Bredon and Littleton,

although it has no upper storey; it has been discreetly restored by the National Trust and retains its original appearance. Set back behind it is Ashleworth Court, a former monastic building of the fifteenth century and still distinctly ecclesiastical in character, with a big entrance arch and a variety of window shapes. The adjacent church has some herringbone masonry and a magnificent old entrance door, but the outstanding feature (apart from what appears to be the worst stained glass in Gloucestershire) is the rood screen in the south aisle, complete with loft floor and steps for access built into the wall. At the west end of the aisle is a huge royal coat of arms of the Tudor period.

For the stranger, the A417 provides the best entry to Gloucester, because there is a convenient car park on the left as soon as you enter the city proper, and since it is quite close to the centre it makes an ideal base for an exploration.

Gloucester has three distinct personalities. It is a cathedral city, a modern commercial centre and a port. Like Worcester, it has suffered from major development which has largely destroyed its medieval character, but it is rather more fortunate in what has been left. The grid of its pre-Norman street plan still exists, and the Cross is still the junction of streets named Northgate, Eastgate, Southgate and Westgate.

In fact Northgate Street and Southgate Street probably follow the line of a Roman road. A legionary fortress, established here soon after the main Roman invasion, was developed into an elaborate civilian settlement and received official town status as Colonia Nervia Glevensis at the end of the first century. The title 'Colonia' indicates a place of considerable importance and there is reason to believe that it was one of the most impressive of the Roman communities, although growth was evidently stunted by the development of nearby Cirencester.

At the beginning of the tenth century, Queen Aethelflaed of Mercia encouraged the foundation of a new settlement within the Roman defences. In the next 200 years it became a centre of royal power and a meeting place for the King and his Council; the Domesday Book was finally planned here in 1085. Four years later work began on a new church for the monastery, the fourth to be built at Gloucester and the basis of the present cathedral. Although the Abbey church acquired cathedral status in 1540, Gloucester's prosperity was largely the result of industrial development in the late eighteenth century, helped later by the creation of an extensive complex of inland docks that made possible a thriving timber and corn trade.

The tour of the town centre which follows starts at the west end of Westgate Street, but since it is a circular walk it can be started at any point on the route.

Walk out of the car park, past the modern flats and into Westgate Street.

Almost at once there is a distinguished timber-framed house on the opposite side of the road. This is Bishop Hooper's Lodging, the house where a Protestant Bishop of Gloucester reputedly spent his last night before being burnt at the stake in 1555. It is a well-restored example of a sixteenth-century group of town houses, now used to accommodate a folk museum. On the other side of the road is St Nicholas' church with its unusual truncated spire (impossible to enter at the time of writing because of building work) and next to it the elaborate Georgian façade of a house that in fact dates from the sixteenth century.

Take the next turning on the left. It is a lane leading to St Mary's Square, a modern but attractive development incorporating a large Victorian monument to Bishop Hooper and the church of St Mary de Lode. (The church is normally kept locked.) What catches the eye here is the ancient St Mary's Gateway leading into the cathedral

Folk Museum, Bishop Hooper's Lodging, Gloucester

precincts. It is an elaborate thirteenth-century structure with stone vaulting, and picturesque houses flank it on each side. As you pass under it and into College Green the dominant impression is of cars; surprisingly parking is permitted right up to the cathedral doors, detracting from what ought to be a secluded close. Nevertheless it is worth touring the perimeter of College Green to study the varied architecture ranging from the sixteenth to the eighteenth centuries. By walking round the west end of the cathedral to Miller's Green it is possible to see the Parliament Room, a fifteenth-century hall grafted on to an earlier stone building. It was originally a monastic house and received its name after a meeting of Parliament there in 1378.

The cathedral itself was begun in 1089 and its nave still retains the enormous strength of the Norman period. The apparent contrast between the plain round pillars and the decorated arches is explained by the fact that new arcading was constructed in the thirteenth century. As usual some of the most interesting monuments are to be found here. A splendid coloured memorial of the early seventeenth century to Thomas Machen and his wife shows seven sons and six daughters mourning them, the younger ones squeezed in rather perfunctorily. There is a stone to Edward Jenner, the pioneer of vaccination, and nearby Sir Onesiphorous Paul is commemorated by a monument that describes his impressive record as a prison reformer. However, the most striking memorial is probably that to Sarah Morley, who died after giving birth to a child during a voyage from India in 1784. The crisp carving by Flaxham shows angels lifting her from the sea with her child in her arms.

After the sobriety of the nave a blaze of colour greets you as you move into the south transept. The tiny chapel of St John the Baptist has been brilliantly restored with medieval tiles on the floor painted emblems on the woodwork and a reredos encrusted with bright colour and gilding. There is further wall painting and another fine reredos in the nearby St Andrew's Chapel, and art of another kind in the painted table tomb of Alderman Blackleech and his wife. This transept is also of great architectural significance in that it was one of the earliest attempts (possibly the first) at what has come to be known as the Perpendicular style.

In the choir, a series of slender columns supporting intricate tracery contrast strongly with the nave and raise the roof 20ft higher. At the west end the organ pipes are finely displayed above the screen, decorated with seventeenth-century painting, while the east end is dominated by the largest stained glass window in England. This is an astounding creation, 78ft high and 38ft wide, dating from 1349 and designed as a triptych with its sides turning in. Its main theme is the Coronation of the Blessed Virgin Mary, and beneath the main group of figures are depicted various kings, saints and martyrs, while lower panels show the shields of many of the knights who fought in the Hundred Years War. Not even the tall and exuberant reredos can detract from the impact of the window. The isolated tomb before the high altar is that of Robert, eldest son of William the Conqueror, whose wooden effigy leaves him in an excruciating cross-legged position.

Back in the south ambulatory is a remarkable example of fifteenth-century joinery — a vast semicircular cope chest.

The size of the east window is even more vividly appreciated as you pass directly beneath it to the entrance of the Lady Chapel. It is built on a large scale, but extensive Victorian restoration has not left much of outstanding interest, apart from the east window where the jumbled glass dates from the fifteenth century. Beneath it the plain reredos is decorated with modern relief panels. There are two or three striking

memorials, the most grandiose being to John Powell, a judge who died in 1713.

The main feature of the north ambulatory is the tomb of Edward II, whose body was brought here following his murder at Berkeley Castle. The beautifully-carved effigy is contained within an intricate stone canopy. Close by, in a wall case, a simple stone cross is an unpretentious reminder of an almost forgotten episode in the Korean War, when a battalion of the Gloucestershire Regiment made a heroic stand at the Imjin river against impossible odds. The cross was carved by their commander, Col J.P. Carne VC, during his period of captivity after the action.

From the north transept, containing another remarkable aldermanic memorial of 1615, it is possible to walk into the cloisters, well worth visiting for their elegant fan vaulting, the earliest surviving example of the style. The Chapter House stands on the east side, but perhaps more notable is a rare example in the north cloister of a monks' lavatorium.

After the cathedral visit the way back to Westgate Street is down College Street, immediately opposite the main door. On leaving the precincts are the remains of the ancient principal entrance, King Edward's Gate. At the end of College Street, note the imposing piece of mock-Tudor on the corner before turning left. Do not miss the next alleyway, because halfway along it is the curious little house chosen by Beatrix Potter as the home of the Tailor of Gloucester; inevitably it has become a Beatrix Potter Centre.

Just before reaching the Cross, Gloucester's commercial hub, turn left into St John's Lane. The church at the top has a typically eighteenth-century appearance and an interior of appropriate elegance, although the tower and spire are fourteenth-century. The lane runs into Northgate Street and away from the Cross, in Hare Lane, Sainsbury's remarkable mural and the medieval buildings on each side of the shop should not be missed. There are two good pubs along here too — the immense Tabard in lordly mock-Tudor and the smaller Imperial, with an outstanding Victorian façade full of ornate patterns and bright green tiling. The Imperial may be preferred to the much-praised New Inn, which is on the left as you walk towards the Cross. It is a fifteenth-century pub with a false front and a picturesque creeper-clad courtyard, but the profusion of signs and olde-worlde decorations give it the apearance of a plastic model. At the Cross, turn left along Eastgate Street to see the splendid Victorian Guildhall in a restrained Italian style, carefully matched by the two adjacent bank buildings. On the other side of the street, the former entrance to the Eastgate market is another refreshing piece of Victoriana.

Amid all the nondescript modern development at the Cross, the tower of St Michael's church has been retained on one corner, and by passing beneath it and turning left into Southgate Street, one of the quaint attractions of Gloucester is reached — the clockmaker's shop with a colourful line of carved figures over the window. They represent John Bull, Father Time, an Irishman, a Scotsman and a Welsh woman, and they each strike a bell as the clock chimes. The fine Jacobean house almost next door was the Berkeleys' town residence.

A handsome range of buildings further down on the right includes the house where Robert Raikes, philanthropist and pioneer of Sunday schools, lived from 1768 to 1801. Its timbering blends harmoniously with the adjacent County Hotel. Redundancy has hit most of the city's old parish churches, but a glorious exception stands almost opposite, and it is worth reserving a generous amount of time to look round St Mary de Crypt.

It is an example of the Perpendicular style widely adopted after its introduction in the cathedral, although it has been much restored and altered both in the nineteenth century and in

recent years. It stands in an attractive setting with big chestnut trees and is a welcome refuge from the traffic. The high arcades and tower arches give an unexpectedly spacious atmosphere to the nave, and the long chancel is equally impressive. The clerestory here was a sixteenth-century addition and the Victorians added the screen, the east window (a copy of medieval glass) and the mosaic reredos, but it all fits harmoniously together. The outstanding feature is the painting on the north wall of the chancel, uncovered in 1842 and showing the Adoration of the Magi as seen by an anonymous sixteenth-century artist. Enough remains to show that it was a rich and accomplished piece of work that must have cost a considerable sum, but there is no hint of the benefactor who paid for it. It has been skilfully restored, and other paintings on the south wall and on each side of the altar await similar treatment.

The flanking chapels have some interesting monuments and there are good brasses in the north transept and aisle. The staircase in this aisle in the leads to the upper floor of the old school room next door which was built in 1539 and now serves as the church hall. Another famous figure associated with St Mary's was George Whitefield, the inspirational eighteenth-century preacher and colleague of John Wesley, and one of the most attractive things at the church is the tiny, tulip-shaped font at which he was baptised. He delivered his first sermons here and the pulpit that he used has been restored.

The path behind the church passes the modern Eastgate market and leads to an area dominated by the technical college, but on the way you pass through Greyfriars, a thirteenth-century foundation with a church of which the nave and north aisle survive, incongruously surrounded by uninspired modern building. The path emerges into Brunswick Road close to the City Museum and Art Gallery; towards the bottom of Brunswick Road there is a

Gloucester Docks

right turn into Parliament Street, where there is an odd mixture of modest cottages in various stages of repair but potentially of great charm; they are on the fringe of the dock area and the street has a waterfront atmosphere about it.

When you reach Southgate Street again cross into Commercial Road, where there is a good view of one of the dock basins. The classical building on the left here is the Customs House, and immediately opposite is Ladybellgate Street, which looks unpromising until Blackfriars, halfway up is reached. It is claimed to be the best-preserved Dominican friary in Britain and was founded at about the same time as the rival Greyfriars. Surrounding buildings make it difficult to appreciate the layout but the significant remains are the church and the cloisters. At the top of Ladybellgate Street the house of the same name presents a most imposing

front, but its old grandeur has now been neutralised by office blocks on a much more brutal scale. Built in 1705, it was later the home of the Raikes family. Its fine interior has been restored in exceptional fashion by the Civic Trust. Two other superb eighteenth-century houses, Bearland House and Bearland Lodge, can be seen by turning left into Longsmith Street.

Berkeley Street leads back from here towards the cathedral, a good example of what can be done to blend old and new architecture. It is an attractive little pedestrian precinct with the seventeenth-century Fountain Inn towards the top. At Westgate Street turn left. Almost immediately you pass the Shire Hall, much altered since its construction in the early nineteenth century but still retaining Robert Smirke's big columned portico.

From here it is a short distance back

The Cathedral
Earliest portions date from 1089 but outstanding feature is work thought to be the first experiment in the Perpendicular style of architecture. East window is the biggest stained glass window in Britain. Also tomb of Edward II.

City Museum and Art Gallery
Brunswick Road
Very wide-ranging displays, including Roman relics and Iron Age mirror. Also furniture, paintings, silver, and natural history.

Folk Museum Bishop Hooper's Lodging, Westgate Street
Reconstructed pin factory, wheelwright's shop and cheese diary, together with smaller exhibits of local life and history.

Regimental Museum The Custom House, Commercial Road
Museum of the Gloucestershire Regiment.

House of the Tailor of Gloucester
College Court
House used by Beatrix Potter as

setting for her famous story. Tableaux and mementoes of the author. Shop.

Pack-Age Albert Warehouse in the Docks
The Robert Opie collection of old-fashioned packets, tins, bottles etc.

Blackfriars Off Ladybellgate Street
Exceptionally well-preserved remains of Friary church.

East Gate Eastgate Street
Gate towers show Roman and medieval work.

Brass Rubbing Centre At the Cathedral
Range of replicas of well-known church brasses.

Antique Centre Severn Road
Converted dock warehouse with every variety of antiques. Reconstructed Victorian shops. Refreshments.

Gloucester Docks
Magnificent warehouses dating from early nineteenth century. Terminal of Gloucester-Sharpness Canal.

to the car park at the end of Westgate Street. The tour will have revealed the extent to which Gloucester has suffered from recent development; as at Worcester there are a good many old buildings remaining, but they have lost their characteristic surroundings and tend to be isolated among modern structures on a totally different scale.

Luckily the same cannot be said about the docks, which remain a priceless asset with unique potential for an inland town. Elizabeth I officially authorised the port in 1580, but there is evidence that the Romans had a quay here, and there was a good deal of water traffic in the middle ages on a channel (now vanished) that lay to the east of the present course of the river. The port was

too close to the rapidly-developing Bristol to be really prosperous, and the extensive complex owes its existence to the Gloucester and Sharpness Canal. This major waterway, designed to obviate the navigational difficulties of the river, was started in 1793, but a series of financial problems and changes of plan delayed its completion until 1827.

The resulting ease of access for large ships enabled Gloucester to become a major distribution point for Irish wheat and Baltic timber. The original docks were expanded in 1849 and 1892, while the construction of deep-water docks at Sharpness led to increased barge traffic. In recent years, however, Avonmouth has monopolised the new container traffic and little commercial activity goes

on now at Gloucester, but there are ambitious plans to develop the area for leisure and cultural purposes, and the fine architectural legacy will no doubt be preserved.

The area is best seen as a series of vistas from the perimeter roads, and a convenient place to start is the Customs House mentioned earlier. It stands close to the original main entrance to the docks in Commercial Road, and despite its 1840 date it has all the elegance of the eighteenth century. The big flour mills close to it date from 1850. Near the junction of Commercial Road and Southgate Street there is a vantage point with a commanding view of the Victoria Dock of 1849; the three main warehouses that line it are appropriately called the Victoria, the Britannia and the Albert and they were all built for the wheat trade, although this dock was also used for loading salt from Droitwich, one of the few products exported from

Gloucester by sea.

Now walk down the lower end of Southgate Street — a rather seedy thoroughfare compared with its upper reaches — and turn in at the next dock entrance past the classical weighbridge office. At the time of writing it is not clear to what extent the public are allowed free access, but since the Albert Warehouse has now become a novel museum of packaging it is at least possible to approach that far, and look at the impressive solidity and pleasing proportions of the warehouses and at the variety of craft in the basin. Here too is the little Mariners' Chapel.

The enthusiast who wants to make a detailed inspection of the wharves with a clear conscience should apply to the British Waterways Board office in Commercial Road for permission. Otherwise continue down Southgate Street and take the next turning on the right (Llanthony Road) which brings you to the lifting bridge at the point where the canal enters the docks. From here is the most striking view of all, along the length of the main basin with the earliest of the warehouses at the top end. It dates from 1826, and those ranged down the right hand side were added in the 1840s. In the other direction the canal (the widest in Britain when it was opened) stretches away past Baker's Quay and the 'Pillar Warehouse'.

Continue along Llanthony Road and turn right into Severn Road, where the river appears on the left, looking oddly irrelevant. This is not the most pleasant road in Gloucester but it provides further views across the main basin and leads to a big warehouse which has already been converted into an 'Antiques Centre'; immediately after it, cross the narrow bridge over the channel giving access to the Severn from the docks, a route still used by quite large craft moving up to Worcester or Stourport. The right turn here leads back to Commercial Road and the starting point of the walk.

In a few years' time this dock area will no doubt be seething with activity once more as it becomes a major tourist attraction, but there is much to be said for visiting it while it still has its unadorned nineteenth-century character and that undefinably exciting atmosphere of the waterfront.

5 Gloucester to Bristol

There is a rather wearisome southwards drive out of Gloucester; back into the city centre, on to the A430 and through two or three miles of suburb before emerging on to the A38 at Hardwicke. The M5, running parallel a mile or so to the east, has created a new boundary between two very different kinds of countryside — the rugged and quite heavily developed Cotswold fringes and the flat, tranquil Vale of Berkeley bordering the Severn estuary to the west. For centuries the Vale has been prosperous agricultural country, largely undisturbed except for the cutting of the Gloucester and Sharpness Canal and, more recently, the building of various industrial installations on the shore of the estuary itself. 'Shore' is a more appropriate word than 'bank' here, because after Gloucester the Severn begins to widen impressively, its narrow navigational channel threading vast areas of sandbank and mud flat.

The atmosphere of Severnside can be sampled by turning right on to the B4071 about five miles after Hardwicke. Very soon Frampton appears on the left, strung out on each side of one of the biggest village greens in Britain. It is generally acknowledged as the Vale's most attractive village, and many visitors will prefer it to some of the better-known Cotswold villages. Frampton Court, built in the 1730s, dominates the eastern side of the green and may be visited by appointment. Its attraction lies in its homely departures from genuine classical design, although its grounds are very ambitious, with a canal, a 'Gothic' orangery and a seventeenth-century dovecote. Facing the Court is a long row of variegated houses, some extremely picturesque, but others nondescript enough to save the

village from prettiness. A walk to the extreme end of the long lane is justified, not only to admire the assorted building styles but to visit the church, which has a rare example of a lead font.

Continuing along the B4071 you enter the 'Arlingham Peninsula', around which the Severn makes its last spectacular meander. Many of the cottages here are built in the distinctive pinkish-grey local brick, seen to advantage at Saul where there is a concentration of former boatmen's houses. The long-disused Stroudwater Canal joined the Severn at Framilode just to the north of Saul; it was built to connect with the Thames and Severn Canal and was the final link in a waterway that connected England's two biggest rivers. It is still possible to trace its course in broken stretches beside the river Frome, which also joins the Severn at Framilode.

These little river and canal communities must have been rough places at one time, and their churches were built late. Those at Fretherne and Framilode date from the middle of the nineteenth century and are not of great interest, although the position of Framilode church, alone and right on the edge of the mud flats, is romantic. Arlingham church should not be missed; it has medieval glass, eighteenth-century chandeliers and some notable monuments.

Those who enjoy solitary walking will note that there are paths beginning and ending at Saul that make possible a ramble round the shore of the peninsula, with a distant prospect of the Forest of Dean on the other side of the river. Another lonely walk begins at Splatt Bridge near Frampton church and can be continued south to the Wildfowl

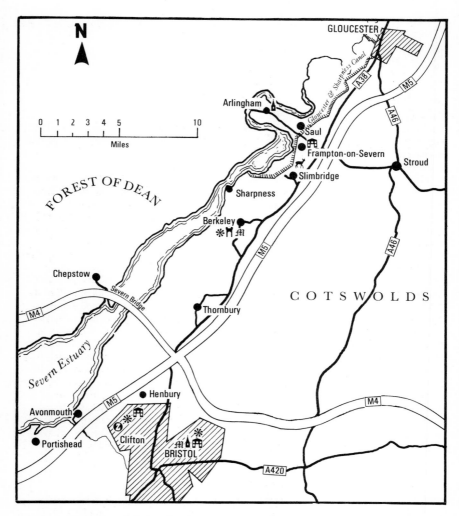

Trust at Slimbridge. It is a rather longer journey for motorists, who need to return to the A38 and drive 3 miles to the Slimbridge turn; the Trust is then a further 2½ miles.

4 miles after the Slimbridge turn, the B4066 leads off to Berkeley, where the castle is the Vale's other celebrated attraction. The town has never developed into the thriving place it might have been, had the builders of the canal to Gloucester carried out their original intention of linking it with the

Severn here. As it is, Berkeley has remained a large village with an enhanced status derived from the castle. There is some pleasant Georgian architecture and the fine Berkeley Arms Hotel, while the parish church is worth visiting for the tombs in the Berkeley Chapel, and the hut nearby in which Edward Jenner conducted his first experiments in smallpox vaccination. A small Jenner museum has been established in Church Lane, in the cottage he gave to his first 'guinea-pig'.

St Mary Redcliffe, Bristol

The Berkeleys have been referred to several times already in connection with Worcester and Gloucester. The family is one of the few that can trace its line reliably back to the Norman Conquest and possibly even further, and it has been in continuous occupation of the castle here since the time of Henry II. Since that time, the castle has undergone many alterations and extensions, and it is now a complex range of buildings. The Norman keep still stands, but is rather outclassed by the fourteenth-century additions, in particular the chapel and magnificent Great Hall. It was at this time that Edward II was murdered in grisly fashion here, and his dungeon can be visited today.

Apart perhaps from a visit to

Sharpness, north of Berkeley, to see the docks and canal terminal, there is little to stop for before the outskirts of Bristol. Coming in on the A38 there is a long stretch of suburbia, including the famous aircraft factory at Filton. For the motorist encountering it for the first time, the centre of Bristol can be an unnerving experience, and it is important to remember that on finally reaching the inner ring road you should turn right. For long-stay parking, the multi-storey car park behind Colston Hall is the most convenient.

The topography of Bristol is as complicated as its history, and it is impossible here to do full justice to either. Fortunately the Information Centre in Colston Street near the car

The Llandoger Trow,
Bristol

park is generous with its literature, and this chapter contains only the basic information needed by the visitor who wants to be sure of seeing what the historic heart of the city has to offer.

Everyone knows that the pre-eminence of Bristol was based on shipping but it is a long way to the sea; incredibly, the town that for centuries was Britain's second busiest port grew up at one end of a seven-mile inlet notorious as a navigational hazard. Mudbanks, awkward tides, fog and the need for laborious towing should have been impossible obstacles, but the commercial acumen and enterprise of the Bristolians provided the indispensable services that made it worth while to ignore all the inconveniences.

It was not until the early nineteenth century that an elaborate series of new engineering works produced an easier channel to the sea and a 'floating harbour' that would not leave ships stranded on the mud at low tide. The innovations came too late to prevent Bristol losing much of the Atlantic trade to Liverpool, but in recent years the development of docks at Avonmouth and Portishead has redressed the balance and Bristol is still a port at one remove.

The city's earlier history, of course, is much more romantic than the unglamorous container trade. It was

---

PLACES OF INTEREST BETWEEN GLOUCESTER AND BRISTOL

Berkeley Castle Berkeley, off A38 12 miles south of Gloucester.
Original keep, fourteenth-century Great Hall, staterooms with fine furnishings and decoration, Edward II's dungeon etc. Grounds.

Jenner Museum Church Lane, Berkeley.
Museum commemorating Edward Jenner, discoverer of smallpox vaccination, in the house which he built for his first 'guinea-pig'.

The Wildfowl Trust On the shore of Severn estuary beyond Slimbridge, off A38 north-east of Berkeley.
180 different species — the world's largest collection of wildfowl.

Frampton Court At Frampton, 5 miles south of Gloucester off A38.
House of 1732 with fine furniture of the period. Impressive gardens, with canal and orangery. Stands in Gloucestershire's most attractive village.

Matson House On south-east outskirts of Gloucester off B4073.
Now Selwyn School. Elizabethan manor house on edge of Robinswood Hill.

Westbury Court Gardens 7 miles south-west of Gloucester on A48.
Historic water garden dating from end of seventeenth century.

England's Mills At Berkeley.
Traditional milling of stone-ground flour.

Ashleworth Court
5 miles north of Gloucester off A417.
Fifteenth-century manor with preserved roof timbers of former Great Hall and other interesting architectural features.

Ashleworth Manor
Notable E-shaped manor house of fifteenth-century date.

Ashleworth Tithe Barn
Well-restored fifteenth-century barn, 120ft long and still in daily use.

Robinswood Hill Country Park
On southern outskirts of Gloucester off B4073.

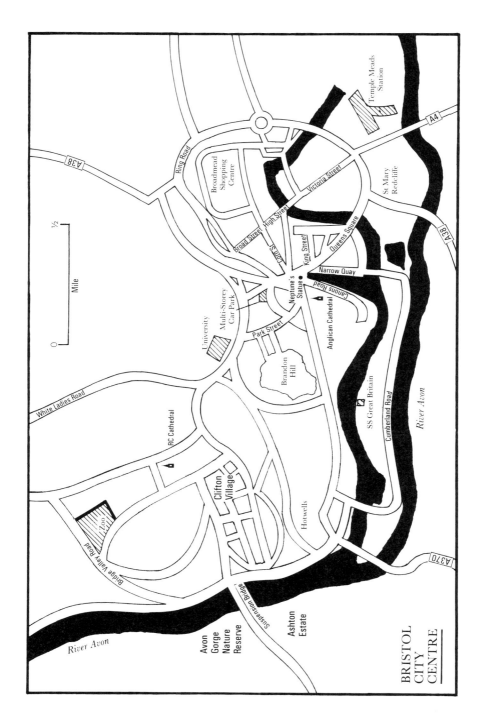

BRISTOL
CITY
CENTRE

Temple Meads Station

A4

St Mary Redcliffe

A38

River Avon

Ring Road

A38

Broadmead Shopping Centre

Victoria Street

High Street

Broad Street

St John's

King Street

Queens Square

Narrow Quay

Canons Road

Neptune's Statue

Multi-Storey Car Park

University

Park Street

Anglican Cathedral

Brandon Hill

SS Great Britain

Cumberland Road

White Ladies Road

RC Cathedral

Clifton Village

Hotwells

Zoo

Bridge Valley Road

Suspension Bridge

Avon Gorge Nature Reserve

Ashton Estate

River Avon

A370

½

Mile

0

from here that Cabot sailed to discover
the continent of North America in 1497,
and it is firmly maintained that America
was named after a Bristol citizen
Richard a Meryck. Just over 100 years
later, Martin Pring and John Guy led
expeditions from Bristol and landed at
Cape Cod and Newfoundland
respectively. William Penn was a Bristol
man whose settlement in Pennsylvania
was a major event in American history.
It is not surprising that a special
commercial relationship with North
America was the basis of Bristol's
prosperity, although wine imports from
Spain and Portugal and heavy
investments in the slave trade proved
equally lucrative.

This legacy of maritime history is
reflected in a unique city centre built
around water, an asset that is now being
busily exploited for the purposes of
leisure and entertainment. The logical
place to start an exploration of the city is
the Neptune statue, which stands gazing
down the narrow arm of water known as
St Augustine's Reach. Behind is the
elongated traffic roundabout known as
The Centre, and in front is an authentic
dockland vista of warehouses and
wharves with a hint of maritime activity
out of sight round the corner.

Start by walking along Narrow Quay
on the left hand side of the Reach. There
is an interesting selection of buildings,
beginning with the monolithic Broad
Quay House, a modern development
happily built in warehouse style, and
ending with a genuine converted
warehouse containing the Arnolfini
Gallery. In between is the less happy
Unicorn Hotel and a multi-storey car
park in intrusive honeycomb style. On
the other side of the Reach is a long row
of low Victorian warehouses
transformed into a leisure complex.
There is a fine view from the end of
Narrow Quay, with the Industrial
Museum across the water directly ahead
and the floating harbour stretching away
on the right.

Turn the corner and walk down

SS Great Britain

Prince Street, once an important
residential thoroughfare, but now
gloomily overhung by bulky buildings.
Just before the Unicorn Hotel there is a
way through on the right that leads into
the vast Queen Square. This is one of the
eighteenth-century showpieces of
Bristol, although it is too big to provide
a unified composition and its design as a
square has been negated by a new main
road running diagonally across it. Some
magnificent buildings remain on the east
side.

Follow the intrusive main road away
from the city centre and out at the south-
east corner of the Square, and continue
to the nearby bridge. This is another fine
viewpoint. To the north is the Welsh
Back section of the harbour — a glimpse
of the old days with its magnificent line
of warehouses, some sadly crumbling —
while to the east Bristol's most famous
church, St Mary Redcliffe, dominates
everything. The busy road system that

cuts off the church needs careful negotiation, but St Mary's is worth the effort. It may be wondered why this huge church should be situated so far away from the city centre, almost as a challenge to the cathedral, and the answer is that Redcliffe developed as a separate settlement and at one time staked a claim to be Bristol's natural centre.

Queen Elizabeth made a famous pronouncement that St Mary Redcliffe was 'the fairest, goodliest and most famous parish church in England'. Certainly it reflects the pride and ambition of Bristol's merchant class with its rich Perpendicular interior, characterised by splendid roof bosses. Naturally there are some impressive tombs here, including that to Admiral Penn, father of the more famous William, and two commemorating William Canynges in his dual capacities as Lord Mayor and priest.

The poets Coleridge and Southey were married in St Mary's, but the church's best-known literary association is with Thomas Chatterton, who was born close by. He lived from 1752 to 1770, and in the course of his short life achieved immense fame as the 'discoverer' of a series of medieval poetic romances about Bristol in which William Canynges figured largely. In fact he produced the poems himself, attributing them to an imaginary monk called Rowley and getting his material from the medieval manuscripts stored in the

muniment room of the church.

After recrossing the bridge walk down Welsh Back, past an interesting array of craft including a lightship from the North Sea that now does duty as a restaurant. The view is closed off by Bristol Bridge, the original crossing point where the earliest settlement grew up, but before that, turn left into King Street, opposite the lightship. The enormous timber-framed pub called the Llandoger Trow makes an immediate impact, as well it might since it comprises three substantial seventeenth-century houses. Inevitably it has come to be identified with the Admiral Benbow in 'Treasure Island'. Its name, incidentally, refers to a type of shallow-draught river barge built at Llandogo, on the Wye north of Chepstow. Note too the more modest pub opposite called The Old Duke; it has a reputation as a jazz venue and appropriately displays Duke Ellington on its sign. If you glance up Queen Charlotte Street that runs beside the Llandoger Trow you will see another building associated in recent years with jazz performances — the huge Old Granary of 1871, a monument to Victorian solidity but with a distinctly frivolous pattern to its bricks.

The remainder of King Street is an array of fine buildings, although its small-scale architecture is diminished by the backdrop of office blocks. Indeed it is difficult to escape the feeling that the street has been preserved under glass, but putting aside this reservation, it is

Bristol Harbour:
Fireworks at the Regatta

possible to enjoy a wide range of buildings here, beginning with the St Nicholas Almshouses of 1656 and the house opposite of the same period with its eight small gables. Beyond them the portico of the Theatre Royal (home of the Bristol Old Vic) marks a successful fusion of two eighteenth-century buildings and a most attractive modern annexe. There is more variety further on, with an interesting group comprising a timber-framed house, an old warehouse and a modern office designed in the 'warehouse style' that seems so popular (and so right) in Bristol. At the far end of King Street, the Merchant Venturers' almshouses for retired seamen are tucked into a corner on the right, a picturesque cluster in pink paint and with a colourful crest.

This walk has taken in the old dock area readily accessible from the city centre, but the visitor wishing to see more of the harbour and the modern waterside development should cross the swing bridge at the end of Narrow Quay and walk down Wapping Road past the Industrial Museum. By turning left at the end you can reach Bathurst Basin, where a range of imaginatively-restored houses look out over the moorings for pleasure craft. To the west, the long Cumberland Road gives access to many attractions. Two features along here of interest to industrial archaeologists are the Fairbairn steam crane of 1875 and a restored dockside locomotive. The Albion Dockyard, further west, has been transformed into a yacht marina with repair facilities. Cumberland Road eventually joins the tangle of new roads around the new bridge at Hotwells, a massive structure designed to swing open when necessary. Here at the Cumberland Basin is the Baltic Wharf Water Leisure Centre, and almost under the bridge itself is a row of attractive dock cottages of 1831.

The foremost attraction in Cumberland Road, however, is the SS Great Britain, still in the process of restoration after being towed from the Falkland Islands in 1970. Her return to Bristol was a triumph, because Isambard Kingdom Brunel designed her here as the world's first iron-clad, screw-driven liner. She made her maiden voyage to New York in 1845 after being launched by Prince Albert. Now she is the centrepiece of a growing Maritime Heritage Centre, which aims to show the working of a major shipyard with the assistance of an extensive collection of plans, documents and artefacts belonging to the firm of Charles Hill.

Back in the city, the Neptune statue is a convenient place to start a tour of the old commercial and residential heart of Bristol. This time move off westwards and cross the road to the Hippodrome, a fine old Edwardian theatre. It stands at one end of a splendid line of buildings known as St Augustine's Parade, which is probably the most varied architectural array in Bristol and certainly the most colourful. On the walk up the Parade, notice the double-gabled house carrying the Tramways Clock, the only reminder now that the city tramway centre occupied the open space in front.   At the end of the Parade, bear left and continue to the top of Colston Street. On the right are the intriguing Foster's Almshouses, a medieval foundation rebuilt in the nineteenth century in an eccentric Hans Andersen style, with whimsical porches, towers and finials and a spiral staircase to the balcony. The building closest to the road is the Chapel of the Three Kings, dating from the fifteenth century and carrying the appropriate statuettes on its façade. Just past the almshouses, walk down Christmas Steps, where a precipitous alleyway lined with small shops has been carefully preserved in all its Dickensian quaintness. The timber-framed houses at the bottom include the thirteenth-century St Bartholomew's Hospital, which was built as an almshouse and later accommodated Bristol Grammar School.

There is a certain incongruity in these preserved relics hemmed in by giant

Bristol Cathedral

---

modern structures, but it would nevertheless be pleasant to see something being done to restore the Lewins Mead Unitarian Chapel, reached by turning left as you join the main street. At the time of writing it is steadily deteriorating in spite of its being a late eighteenth-century building, and potentially the most distinguished in the neighbourhood. Cross the road in front of it and walk round the back of the modern block forming an island on the left. On the other side of Nelson Street, St John's Gate provides access to Broad Street.

Broad Street marks a return to a more intimate environment. St John's Gate is the only surviving gateway of the medieval town, and it supports the tower of St John's Church which is built on the town walls. A little further up on the left is the unique Edward Everard building — a printer's shop of 1900 decorated with Art Nouveau tiled illustrations of the printer's craft. An angel in the centre is flanked by Gutenberg on one side and

William Morris on the other. There is a surprise just beyond it at the end of a narrow alleyway called Tailor's Court; it is St John's churchyard, totally enclosed and regrettably dismal. This same alley contains the hall of the Merchant Tailors' Guild with its fine hooded doorway and a striking medieval house built over the entrance arch. At the top of Broad Street the site of the former High Cross is the hub of Bristol's old commercial centre.

Christ Church stands on one corner and should not be missed. Erected in the 1780s, it is a classic Georgian church, discreetly white and gold inside with slender columns and a vaulted ceiling. Wine Street (heavily bombed during the war) leads north-east from here, giving access to the Broadmead Shopping Centre. It is not at all attractive, but a visit is recommended because it incorporates Britain's first Methodist chapel, John Wesley's New Room. Built in 1739, it is a fascinating place; a ground-floor chapel with galleries and

PLACES OF INTEREST IN BRISTOL

The Cathedral College Green
Medieval east end, nineteenth-
century nave. Very much underrated
among English cathedrals.
Magnificent Norman chapter house
and Eastern Lady Chapel, Berkeley
Chapel, medieval carving in Elder
Lady Chapel and many other features
of particular interest.

St Mary Redcliffe South-east of city
centre.
Outstanding example of
Perpendicular architecture with
notable roof. Many interesting
memorials.

John Wesley's New Room Preserved
in modern Broadmead shopping
centre.
The first of Wesley's chapels, built in
1739. Beautiful interior design with
upper rooms occupied by Wesley and
colleagues. Museum items.

City Museum and Art Gallery Queen's
Road.

Bristol's main museum with very
comprehensive collections to appeal
to all ages and tastes. Shop and
refreshments.

St Nicholas' Church Museum St
Nicholas Street.
Distinguished church now housing
exhibitions explaining early history
of Bristol. Also specialist collections
of church plate and vestments.

Industrial Museum Prince Street.
Exhibits illustrating industrial history
of Bristol, including wide range of
vehicles, machinery, aero-engines,
model railways etc. Famous
Fairbairn steam crane nearby.

SS Great Britain Off Cumberland
Road.
Centrepiece of new Maritime
Heritage Centre. Brunel's
experimental ship, the first iron-clad,
propeller-driven liner, retrieved from
Falkland Islands in 1970. Still under
restoration but can be visited.

---

fine staircases leading to a two-decker
pulpit and the living quarters of Wesley
and his associates on the first floor.

High Street, the continuation of
Broad Street, also suffered heavily from
war damage and hardly lives up to its
name now. It leads to Bristol Bridge,
and has at its back the landscaped Castle
Park, once the site of the castle that was
established close to the river crossing. At
the far end of High Street by the bridge,
the church of St Nicholas has been
converted into a museum specialising in
local archaeology, church plate and
vestments.

The fourth arm of the crossroads is
the imposing Corn Street, Bristol's
financial centre, which is very
reminiscent of the City of London. The
eighteenth-century Exchange on the left
is noticeable because of the 'nails' in
front of it. They are circular bronze

pillars with flat tops which merchants
used as tables to exchange payments,
thus 'paying on the nail'. A lane down
the side leads to St Nicholas' Market
where a remarkable variety of stalls can
be found. The Grecian frontage beyond
the Exchange belongs to the
Commercial Rooms, built in 1811 as a
merchants' club and later equipped with
one of the early telegraph systems to give
notice of the arrival of ships. The rest of
Corn Street is lined by severe banks and
offices, although the ornate Venetian
façade of Lloyd's Bank provides light
relief.

Just before Corn Street joins the
Centre, a road to the right leads to the
final stop on this walk: St Stephen's, the
central parish church of Bristol. Its
immensely tall tower no longer
dominates as it used to, but its
splendidly-embellished interior contains

National Lifeboat Museum
Prince Street.
Museum of the Royal National
Lifeboat Institution.

Blaise Castle House At Henbury,
northern outskirts of Bristol.
Museum of West Country life.
Grounds contain iron age fort and
'Gothick castle.

The Georgian House 7 Great George
Street.
Late eighteenth-century house
restored and furnished as example of
affluent household of the period.

The Red Lodge Park Row.
Suite of sixteenth-century rooms and
eighteenth-century modifications.
House was used as first girls'
reformatory.

Lord Mayor's Chapel College Green.
Unusual in being owned by
Corporation since sixteenth century.
Notable for French and Flemish
stained glass and Spanish tiles.

King Street
'Preserved street' containing range of
buildings of many periods.

Watershed Canons Road.
Cinemas, exhibition galleries, shops,
restaurants etc in single quayside
complex.

Arnolfini Narrow Quay.
Multi-media arts centre with
restaurant, shops etc.

Albany Centre Shaftesbury Avenue,
Montpelier.
Community Arts Centre with multi-
ethnic emphasis. Arts performances
and instructional workshops.

Brass Rubbing Centre
At St Nicholas' Church Museum.

Brandon Hill
Open space to west of city centre.
Panoramic views over city, docks and
Clifton. Cabot Tower on summit can
be climbed.

some of the city's most notable
memorials. One of the most flamboyant
is to Sir George Snygge who died in
1617, and there is a much smaller but
beautifully ornate wall memorial to
Martin Pring, discoverer of Cape Cod.
Notice also the fine seventeenth-century
wrought-iron gates.

The third walk moves away from the
ancient nucleus of the city towards the
more spacious area west of the centre,
the district that includes the cathedral
and the university. Once again the
Neptune statue can be the starting point,
but you need to walk towards St
Augustine's Parade and take the road
that curves away uphill. After a sharp
rise it emerges on College Green, a huge
triangular space with the Cathedral on
one side and the massive civic buildings
on another. Everything looks different
up here — almost as if Bristol had an

upstairs floor — and in these expansive
surroundings it is easy to imagine what a
tight and unhealthy huddle the low-lying
old town must once have been.

The cathedral has never ranked in the
same league as Salisbury or Winchester,
but it proves unexpectedly rewarding.
The ancestors of the ubiquitous Berkeley
family first established an Augustinian
abbey here in 1140, but the present
structure is the result of steady
rebuilding and addition well into the
Victorian age (the twin west towers were
completed in 1888).

The nave dates from 1868, and was
the work of G.E. Street, who followed
the foundations of an unfinished nave of
the early sixteenth century. Since he
matched the height of the existing east
end and adopted the same architectural
style, the cathedral has an unusual unity
of design. Two interesting memorials

can be seen in the nave: a florid monument to Sir John and Lady Young (1606) and one in more restrained style to Sir Charles Vaughan. Note also the windows in the north wall portraying the home defence services of World War II. At the tower crossing the carved stone screen with brass gates (1904) marks the end of Street's work; the tower and transepts are of the fifteenth century. The north transept is unremarkable except for the memorials to Bishop Butler and to a nineteenth-century journalist (the latter complete with pewter inkwell and quill pen), but the adjoining Elder Lady Chapel is noted for some cheerful medieval carving of birds and animals, with monkeys unaccountably predominating.

The Choir has been much altered and restored, but the roof is original and a striking example of a distinctive technique in medieval architecture — instead of meeting a straight ridge-rib (as in the nave) the vaulting is dispersed in patterns at its apex. The sanctuary is a typically rich Victorian reconstruction with an elaborate white stone reredos and a marble floor patterned with kaleidoscopic effect. The stalls, however, retain their carving of about 1500 and there are some intriguing misericords.

The eastern Lady Chapel is magnificent in its colour and gilding. The reredos, almost Byzantine in character, is echoed in the highly unusual wall niches surmounted by star-shaped arches, and the windows have restored fourteenth-century glass. The whole effect is unbelievably exotic. Most of the heraldic features here relate to the Berkeleys, and as you move into the south choir aisle, you glimpse their own chapel through huge niches in the same star shape. The chapel (entered through a sacristy that has the remains of an oven used for baking Communion bread) contains a rare medieval chandelier and unusual twin altars. Before leaving the south choir aisle note the abstract stained glass window at the east end, symbolising the Holy Spirit as

light and fire. The south transept houses the Newton Chapel, packed with monuments, but the most interesting feature here is a superb example of a Saxon coffin lid on the wall.

It is through a door from this transept that one passes into the cloister leading to the famous Norman chapter house. It is difficult to believe that the richness of decoration here could have been achieved solely by the repeated carving of simple patterns on the vaulting and on those parts of the wall not embellished with blind arcading. The chapter house has justifiably been called the finest Norman room in Britain. The original gateway to the abbey stands just to the west of the cathedral. It was built over in the sixteenth century with handsome results, but perhaps more interesting is the adjoining library, designed in the early years of this century to harmonise with its neighbour.

The crescent-shaped civic buildings are best admired from a distance. They are a good example of the sort of early postwar architecture that tried to be both conservative and mildly adventurous and they are not universally popular. Certainly the central porch looks like an afterthought, but generally the clean straight lines give solidity and dignity, while the lofty arches at each end add just enough interest. The third side of the triangular College Green is made up of a variety of smaller buildings of which the gem is the Lord Mayor's Chapel. Technically it is the church of St Mark, but it has been owned by the Corporation since 1541. You step down into a dark, compact interior with a wooden roof painted dramatically in black and gold and lit through French and Flemish glass of the sixteenth century. Spanish tiles of the same period can be seen in the Poyntz Chapel in the south aisle, where there is a rich collection of monuments.

The next part of the walk involves a good deal of climbing, beginning with the steep and busy Park Street. At one time this was a rather select shopping centre, but the proximity of the university at the top has given it a 'student quarter' air with plenty of small restaurants and bookshops. Just over halfway up the hill turn left into Great George Street, which has a number of gracious Georgian houses, including one that has been preserved as a domestic museum of the period. In this street, too, is the elegant St George's Church of 1823 at the top of its imposing steps; the interior has been splendidly refurbished and music recitals are frequently staged here.

At the top of the street turn right and continue climbing to the point where there is a fine view down the Regency terrace of Charlotte Street. A gate leads on to Brandon Hill, one of the best vantage points in Bristol. It is possible to climb even higher, to the top of Cabot Tower, erected in 1897 to commemorate the great explorer, but this is not

necessary in order to enjoy the panorama beneath, especially the views over the harbour to the south with the SS Great Britain prominent in the foreground. Go round the hill to the north side, passing on the way the earthworks of defences prepared during the Civil War, and descend through the 'specimen' trees into Berkeley Square, which is Regency again and now largely the preserve of the university. By walking the long way round the square you emerge into Queen's Road.

The first surprise here is the sight of the long façade of a big department store, apparently isolated from any of the main shopping centres, but the university buildings soon catch the attention. The most prominent at this point is the refectory of 1872, originally the Bristol Museum and Library and startlingly Italianate in design; indeed, it is said to have been inspired by the

The Avon Gorge, Clifton Suspension Bridge

Royal York Crescent, Clifton – 'the most romantic street in Europe'

Doge's Palace in Venice. Equally flamboyant is the University Tower down Park Row to the right. It looks Victorian but in fact dates from 1925, when it was created as a memorial to H.O. Wills, the university's greatest benefactor in its early days. The comparatively sober exterior of the City Museum and Art Gallery nearby hides a most lively and varied range of displays; there are scholarly collections relating to ancient history, Egyptology, porcelain and glass, but also odd corners and landings can be found containing a gypsy caravan or a row of old pianos.

Continue the walk down Park Row, along Perry Road to where St Michael's Hill climbs away steeply on the left. The Colston Almshouses are situated on the hill — a charming group set round three sides of a square with a central chapel, all dating from 1691. As a final call before returning to the city centre, walk back along Perry Road to the Red Lodge, which contains a fine suite of sixteenth-century rooms with magnificent panelling. The Lodge, which is open to the public, bears a plaque recording the fact that Lord Byron's widow bought it to enable Mary Carpenter to establish the first girls'

reformatory in 1854.

These three walks do not, of course, exhaust the pleasures of Bristol. It is unfortunately not possible here to describe in detail the historic inner suburbs, but one district that cannot be ignored is Clifton, the elegant 'village' that lies above the Avon Gorge to the west of the city.

Its development was closely involved with that of Hotwells, the riverside spa that was immensely popular during the eighteenth-century. It occupied an area to the north of the Cumberland Basin, and as it attracted more and more visitors it was natural that hotels and boarding houses should be opened on the healthy slopes above it, and equally natural that the wealthier residents of Bristol should want to move into these pleasant and genteel surroundings. During the nineteenth century, Clifton spread rapidly northwards over the downs and, like Cheltenham and Leamington, became a popular place for retirement. Additional status was conferred on it by the opening of a major public school, Clifton College, in the 1860s. Nowadays it has declined in gentility and has acquired a bohemian air from the nearby university, but its

impressive streets and fine situation
certainly repay a visit.

Clifton Village, the older quarter, can
be reached quickly by following Queen's
Road, to the west of the university, but
the more interesting route is by way of
Hotwells. From the city centre take the
road that passes the cathedral. You will
recognise Hotwells by the miniature
Spaghetti Junction at Plimsoll Bridge,
where you make for the Avonmouth
road. (Anyone wishing to explore what
is left of the old spa will find a
convenient car park under the flyovers.)
The road now runs above the Gorge and
passes under the famous suspension
bridge, providing an opportunity to
appreciate the miraculous delicacy of
Brunel's design. Shortly after the bridge
branch right for the steep climb up
Bridge Valley Road and on to the
downs. This road brings you quickly to
Bristol Zoo on the right, while on the left
are the broad expanses of Clifton Down
and Durdham Down.

Clifton Village lies to the south, and
the best route is probably College Road,
which runs beside the Zoo grounds; a
road to the left just after the College
leads to the Roman Catholic Cathedral
of St Peter and St Paul, completed in
1973 to a brilliant design with an equally
exciting interior that makes it one of
Britain's best modern ecclesiastical
buildings. In the Village the streets that
lie between Victoria Square and the
Gorge are full of fine Regency terraces
like Cornwallis Crescent and Royal
York Crescent (the longest Georgian
crescent in England). Sion Hill forms
their western boundary, curving and
climbing to the Suspension Bridge.

This spectacular engineering work is
one of Bristol's foremost attractions.
Brunel won the design competition in
the 1830s but died before it finally
opened in 1864, and was thus never able
to see how fully it embodied his belief
that a bridge here should not be allowed
to intrude on the natural beauty of the
Gorge. The structure is light, splendidly-
proportioned and totally simple. It can
be driven over, but it is a pity not to
enjoy the views by walking across to the
open country on the other side, where
the wooded Avon Gorge Nature Reserve
lies to the north and the public Ashton
estate to the south.

There is one remaining Bristol
showpiece, to be taken in perhaps on the
return journey from the city. The Blaise
Castle Estate is at Henbury, about a mile
from the M5, and can be most easily
reached from Clifton by following the
road past the Zoo and through
Westbury on Trym and then taking the
B4055 on the left. Blaise Castle House is
an outpost of the city museum service,
and the dignified eighteenth-century
mansion contains a pleasant collection
of folk exhibits, both rural and urban.
The castle is a 'Gothic' folly and the
main feature of the fine gardens, but
there is also a famous group of estate
cottages designed by John Nash in a self-
consciously picturesque style.

From here it is a drive of 2 miles to the
nearest junction of the M5.

6 Leamington Spa, Kenilworth and Warwick

For most visitors an exploration of the Avon will begin with these three famous Warwickshire towns. Although they lie very close together, they each have an individual character that prevents their becoming an amorphous conurbation, and several full days could be spent in enjoying the variety they offer.

Leamington Spa is the youngest. Its name has become a symbol of upper-middle-class respectability, so it comes as a surprise to find a busy commercial and manufacturing centre with a cosmopolitan population. Extensive recent development, however, has done nothing to erase the town's personality, exemplified in a spacious layout, elegant terraces and squares, wide streets, leafy avenues and dignified architecture.

Leamington was a late but quick developer. In 1800 it was a village with little more than 300 inhabitants. One or two of the saline springs that were to make its fortune had been discovered in the 1780s, notably by Benjamin Satchwell, who was the first to publicise them. In 1814 Henry Jephson, a local doctor, opened the Pump Rooms next to the river Leam offering curative treatments. It was the charisma of Jephson that attracted aristocratic patronage in the early nineteenth century, and the town's reputation was enhanced by the conferring of Royal status by Queen Victoria.

When the spa cult faded, Leamington retained its vitality by being adaptable. It was already a fashionable shopping centre, but industrial development in post-war Coventry brought other opportunities, including ancillary factories and a big influx of commuters. In fact it has never ceased to be a spa; its treatment centre is now an integral part of the National Health Service and deals with many thousands of patients annually.

The Pump Room is an appropriate

PLACES OF INTEREST IN AND AROUND LEAMINGTON SPA

Chesterton Windmill 1 mile west of Harbury, 4 miles south-east of Leamington off A425.
Notable stone-built mill of 1632.

All Saints Church
Imposing example of nineteenth-century Gothic style.

Town Hall The Parade.
Outstanding Victorian civic building in extravagant style.

Newbold Comyn On eastern outskirts of town.
Former estate of Willes family. Good walking, golf and other sports facilities.

Art Gallery and Museum Avenue Road.
Good permanent collection, particularly of Dutch, Flemish and modern work. Fine glass and porcelain.

Jephson Gardens
Extensive and very attractive riverside gardens. Lake, aviary, tearoom.

Southam Zoo 5 miles east of Leamington on A425.
Small zoo noted for big cats. Pets corner.

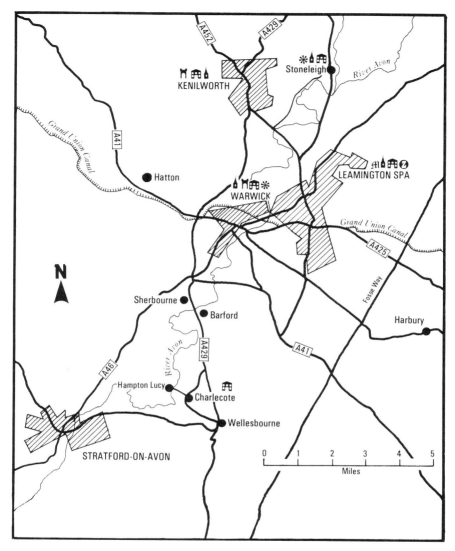

place to start a walk. It is not the imposing building you might expect, but its present clean-cut façade with a fine colonnade is deceptive. The design seems to be classical Regency, but photographs from the 1950s show it with an ungainly tower at one corner and a multitude of embellishments at roof level. They were added in 1862, and their subsequent removal must be counted an improvement. The modest front conceals quite a large complex overlooking the pleasant riverside park at the rear.

Its most prominent neighbour is the church of All Saints, one of Britain's largest and most impressive parish churches. The site was originally occupied by a twelfth-century chapel of ease, but the rapidly-growing town

A Regency house in Leamington Spa

demanded something grander, and in 1843 the Rev John Craig inaugurated the building of this massive example of Victorian Gothic. It took a long time to complete, and the final stage — the tower — was not added until the turn of the century. It follows that the church contains nothing of great historical interest, but the Anglo-Catholic tradition of worship has resulted in a most sumptuous interior, the outstanding feature being a magnificent rose window in the south transept.

Return over the bridge and through the gates between the two small lodges opposite the Pump Room (one of them is the Information Centre). This is the entrance to one of Leamington's greatest assets, the Jephson Gardens. There was a public open space here in 1836, but as a tribute to Henry Jephson additional land was acquired from the Willes family and the present gardens established in 1848. They contain just about everything one could wish for: lawns, flowerbeds, fine trees, a lake with fountains, a pavilion for tea and the river running by. They are heavily used but manage to keep their air of Victorian distinction.

It is possible to leave the gardens at the far end, at Willes Road, where a left turn brings you to Lansdowne Circus, a tight circle of delightful small houses of 1835. Nathaniel Hawthorne, the American writer, lived here for a time at No 10, and his own description still conveys the character of the Circus: 'One of the cosiest nooks in England....a circular range of pretty, moderate-sized, two-storied houses, all built on nearly the same plan and each provided with a little grass plot, its flowers, its tufts of box framed into cubes and other fantastic shapes, and its verdant hedges shutting the house in from the common

Kenilworth Castle

Eastgate, Warwick

The River Avon at Charlecote Park

Wooton Wawen

Town Centre, Leamington Spa

drive and dividing it from its equally
cosy neighbours.'

The little enclave is tucked away at
one end of Lansdowne Crescent, one of
Leamington's best Regency terraces.
From here continue straight along
Warwick Street to the Parade. From this
point there is an excellent view of what is
probably the most handsome shopping
street in the Midlands. It was designed to
impress and it still does, with an
immensely long sweep of dignified
frontages sloping down almost to the
Pump Room. Turn right and walk
towards the top. You pass in front of a
terrace that looks authentic but is in fact
a modern reproduction; only the
Clarendon Hotel at the far end is
original, dating from 1836.

A few hundred yards from the top of
the Parade is Clarendon Square, another
of the town's showpieces. Expansive in
design and built around a large central
garden, it has considerable architectural
variety. The west side was obviously
intended to be superior, judging by the
private drive, the screen of trees and the
very fine ironwork. The notorious
Aleister Crowley, dabbler in the occult,
was born at No 30 Clarendon Square
and Napoleon III spent some time at No
6 while in exile.

There is more impressive architecture
in Clarendon Place, which leads
downhill from the south-west corner of
the Square along the western edge of
Leamington's grid layout. Cross
Warwick Street and turn left into Regent
Street, which is a more humdrum
commercial thoroughfare with an
interesting mixture of smaller buildings.
At its junction with the Parade turn
right. Dominating the opposite side of
the Parade are the Regent Hotel and the
Town Hall, each in its own way
symbolising the spa's past grandeur. The

97

Castle Green, Kenilworth

Regent opened in 1819 as the William Hotel and was the largest hotel in England at the time. Very soon afterwards the Prince Regent visited the town and was sufficiently impressed to give the hotel its present name. Its elegant symmetry is in striking contrast to the eccentricity of its neighbour. In fact it is difficult to know what to say about this late-Victorian extravaganza, which appears to have been designed by assembling in random order all the illustrations from a history of architecture. It is an endearing building, and Leamington can easily tolerate this kind of outrageous individuality.

At the lower side of the Town Hall, Regent Grove defies the grid plan by leaving the Parade at an angle. It was created in 1829 by the Willes family as a carriage drive from the town centre to their mansion at Newbold Comyn, just to the east of the town. It contains some exceptional Victorian houses and is a reminder that the Newbold Comyn estate is nowadays a public recreation centre.

The name occurs again a little further down, where the splendid Newbold Terrace runs alongside the Jephson Gardens. Some of its large Victorian villas can still be seen, and Newbold

Street, which leads from it halfway along, is another example of Leamington's Regency style.

This walk will have revealed some of the attractions of the 'new' town centre that developed with Leamington's rapid recognition as a leading spa, but the original settlement was on the south side of the river behind All Saints' church. Nothing now remains of the old village of Leamington Priors, but the earliest surviving buildings can be seen by crossing the bridge, turning left into Priory Terrace and then right into George Street and Mill Street. Satchwell Place dates from 1805, and the streets around it represent the very early development away from the original nucleus where the mineral springs were situated.

Effective landscaping has turned the modest river Leam into an asset. After running through the Jephson Gardens it continues west to join the Avon and provides a pleasant stroll by way of a bridge behind the Pump Room and a riverside walk that extends into Victoria Park. The circuit of the Park leads into Park Drive and Avenue Road, where there is a chance to visit the museum and art gallery.

A more ambitious walk (marked on

the OS map) begins at the entrance to Newbold Comyn (151:330659), continues west across the former Willes estate for a mile, crosses the Leam and passes through the park of Offchurch Bury into the pleasant village of Offchurch. An alternative return is by way of the path beginning at 151:364655, which crosses a disused railway and joins the Fosse Way. Half a mile to the south the towpath of the Grand Union Canal leads back into Leamington.

It is a quick drive to Kenilworth along the main road, but a diversion through Stoneleigh provides a more interesting route. Shortly after leaving Leamington on the A452 turn on to the Coventry Road, and after 3 miles take the left turn for Stoneleigh. The National Agricultural Centre is situated here and once a year it is the scene of the massive Royal Show, but it also stages events at other times and it is worth enquiring about the programme.

The showground is part of the Stoneleigh Abbey estate. A disastrous fire in 1960 destroyed much of this celebrated house, but the present Lord Leigh has determinedly set out to restore it, and now the riverside gardens and ten rooms of the house are open to the public. The first buildings here were part of a twelfth-century monastery, although only the gatehouse and an undercroft (now a restaurant) remain from this period. The present house is part Elizabethan and part eighteenth-century. Some fine plasterwork and panelling survived the fire, and other outstanding features are the staircase, the Saloon, the library and the exquisitely-decorated bedroom used by Queen Victoria in 1858.

Stoneleigh itself was no doubt once a lively and bustling estate village, but the cottages have now become prim and immaculate under new ownership. They exemplify a range of styles — brick, timber, thatch and at least one cruck cottage opposite the post office. Amid the extreme neatness, the blacksmith's shop is allowed to be picturesquely

untidy on the little village green. St Mary's church, though, is a gem. The exterior shows Norman traces, including an interesting tympanum over the north door, and the interior is dominated by what must surely be the finest Norman chancel arch in the county. Apart from the elaborate carving on the arch itself the piers are finely decorated and have some homely individual touches. The chancel contains a huge black and white marble monument to Duchess Dudley, who died in 1688, and there is a sandstone memorial to an anonymous priest. The font, bearing carvings of the twelve apostles, is Norman and the church fittings are completed by some exceptional early nineteenth-century woodwork.

Kenilworth can now be reached by taking the B4115 and joining the A452. Approaching from this southerly direction you enter the town through the shopping centre that looks like any suburban High Street, and the modern development of Kenilworth is neatly symbolised at the top, where a Victorian clock tower is incongruously dwarfed by the huge de Montfort Hotel behind it. Turn left here and follow the signs to the castle, where there is a large car park.

The extensive ruins in warm red stone are the result of action by Oliver Cromwell's men, who held it after the battle of Edgehill and did their best to render it useless when they left it. Building started in the twelfth century, and the original keep survives, but as usual the castle was modified and extended with notable additions by John of Gaunt. It figured largely in Simon de Montfort's rebellion against Henry III; de Montfort had acquired it on marrying Henry's sister, and following his death at the battle of Evesham in 1265 his son garrisoned the castle against the royal forces, enduring a six-month siege before surrendering. It remained in royal possession until 1563, when Elizabeth gave it to her favourite Robert Dudley, who entertained her lavishly there in 1575.

PLACES OF INTEREST IN AND AROUND KENILWORTH

The Castle
Original twelfth-century keep with later alterations and additions, notably by John of Gaunt. Extensive remains.

Abbey and Abbey Barn Abbey Fields. Slight remains of abbey, but best of its stonework is preserved in Abbey Barn, together with various exhibits of local interest.

Stoneleigh Abbey 2 miles east of Kenilworth on B4115.
Recently reopened after fire damage.

Basically eighteenth-century house with earlier elements, including medieval undercroft and gatehouse. Fine staterooms. Landscaped grounds contain walks and childrens' amusements.

Royal Showground In grounds of Stoneleigh Abbey.
Royal Show held here in early July, and also other events open to public.

Crackley Wood 1 mile north of Kenilworth.
Nature trail.

Visitors enter along a causeway that once crossed a lake. It partly encircled the castle to the south and was one of its most formidable defences. The Parliamentarians deliberately destroyed the dam that created it, and now the lake bed to right and left of the causeway is used as cattle pasture. A detailed guide to the castle is available, indeed essential to understand the complex ruins that include the Keep, John of Gaunt's

banqueting hall and some of Dudley's additions, in particular the fine four-storey gatehouse.

Old Kenilworth is separated from the new development by Abbey Fields to the east of the castle, and it is possible to walk through them to reach St Nicholas' church, which had a substantial Victorian restoration that left little of great interest apart from the fine Norman west doorway. Close by are the

Leycester's Stables, Courtyard of Kenilworth Castle

Mill Street, Warwick

ruins of Kenilworth Abbey, founded in 1122 and now virtually reduced to its foundations. The Abbey Barn contains good examples of the stonework as well as other archaeological finds and some agricultural exhibits. Also worth visiting are Little Virginia, a group of cottages at the east end of the High Street (traditionally the site of the first planting of Raleigh's Virginia potatoes) and Castle Green, a well-restored row of small houses just outside the castle walls to the east.

A good walk through the open countryside to the west of Kenilworth begins at a gate on the west side of the castle car park. It starts on a track and after half a mile branches left on to a footpath running north of Fernhill Farm. Branch left again at 140:266709 and follow the path south for nearly a mile before turning sharp right on to a bridleway that joins a metalled track at 140:251705. Follow this lane to Hill Farm and turn right for th return to the car park. This walk is one of several possibilities in this area, all clearly marked on the OS map.

It is now time to move on to Warwick. Leave Kenilworth on the A452, then take the A46 and branch off for the town centre after about three miles. Once in the town you are strongly recommended to follow the signs for Banbury, cross

Warwick Castle

*The Lord Leycester
Hospital, Warwick*

the junction at the castle gates and turn left immediately afterwards into St Nicholas' Park, just before the river bridge. This is not only a pleasant place to leave the car, but also a good starting-point for an exploration of the town.

It seems odd to begin in a suburb, but few tourists bother to walk round Bridge End, one of Warwick's most charming quarters. It is reached by crossing the river bridge (there is a famous view of the castle from here) and turning right. With its mixture of black and white and old brick cottages, and its tranquil air Bridge End can rival any Warwickshire village. Return over the bridge, walk up to the castle gates and down the road just to the left of them. This is Mill Street, and its profusion of timber-framed houses with the castle looming above gives some idea of what Warwick must once have looked like.

One of the crucial events in the town's history was a disastrous fire in 1694 which changed the whole character of the centre. The Saxon settlement here was created by the daughter of King Alfred, and the town developed steadily with the building of a castle in 1086 and the later influence of the powerful Beauchamp family. But the fire swept away most of the huddled medieval buildings, and apart from the occasional survival, as here in Mill Street, most

buildings in Warwick are of stone, or at least stone-faced.

In recent years the castle has become the centrepiece for visitors to Warwick. It has had an eventful history. Apart from the motte, there are few traces now of the Norman castle of the mid-eleventh century, and the present buildings date substantially from the fourteenth century when the Earldom of Warwick passed to the Beauchamps. Their sophisticated work was completed by the five-storey Guy's Tower of 1395. Following the rebellion and defeat of Richard Neville (Warwick the Kingmaker), ownership passed to the Crown, and Elizabeth later gave it to Ambrose Dudley, brother of Robert Dudley who received Kenilworth Castle. Up to this time the castle had been primarily a military fortress, but when it came into the possession of Lord Brooke in 1604 work began on converting it into a stately home, and apart from an interruption during the Civil War this process has continued. In 1978 it was sold to Madame Tussaud's, who set about turning it into a more calculated tourist attraction.

There have been two main results; the development of ancillary attractions such as picnic areas, a childrens' playground, a woodland walk and medieval banquets, and a more

102

theatrical approach to the buildings themselves. Thus in the state apartments you can now see a reconstruction of a Victorian house party complete with waxwork figures. It is all quite seemly and entertaining despite what the purists may say.

From the gates walk along Castle Lane and bear right into Castle Street. The half-timbered building here is Oken's House, and it has been well restored inside and out to accommodate an interesting doll museum. Castle Street joins Jury Street, the eastern end of the main thoroughfare that shows off the town's Georgian and Victorian architecture. Turn left here and walk towards the Westgate. There is much to admire on both sides of the street, but Albion House and the Lord Leycester Hotel are outstanding. Westgate is the site of a very fine group of timber-framed buildings that escaped the fire and now press in on each side of the narrow gate.

Dominating the scene is the famous Lord Leycester Hospital, its irregular structure beautifully restored to something approaching authenticity. It was founded by Robert Dudley (later Earl of Leicester) as a place of retirement for old soldiers in 1571, but before that the buildings had served as the headquarters of three town Guilds, and also for a short time as the grammar school. It is still occupied by retired soldiers and their wives, so much of it is not open to the public, but visitors can walk round the attractive courtyard and see some of the main rooms, including the Great Hall where James I was entertained, the Guildhall and the regimental museum of the Queen's Own Hussars, which is housed in the former Chaplain's Dining Hall.

If you now walk through the Westgate and turn right a pleasant group of buildings including a distinctive Victorian school can be seen. Continue up Market Street and into the market place, where the former market hall is islanded. It is now the county museum. Prominent at the other end of the square is the new Shire Hall; it has incorporated

St Mary's Church, Warwick. The Beauchamp Chapel, with the tombs of Richard Beauchamp and Ambrose Dudley.

some good earlier buildings, notably a fine town house called Abbotsford (at the corner of the Square) and an eighteenth-century house at the back of Northgate Street. It is worth walking to the top of Northgate Street to see Northgate House, which dates from 1698 and is a curious example of early semi-detached design with a central carriage gate.

St Mary's church lies at the bottom of Northgate Street. It is one of the great sights of Warwick, not so much because of its exterior (the nave and tower were rebuilt after the fire) but because so much of value has survived inside. The original collegiate foundation was established here in 1123, but only the crypt remains of the first Norman work. The other pre-eighteenth century portions are the fourteenth-century choir and the Beauchamp Chapel, which was started in 1442 and took many years to complete.

The pinnacled tower, 170ft high, was splayed across the pavement as a way of securing a firmer foundation. Advice on this matter was given by one of Sir Christopher Wren's assistants, but there is no truth in the widely-held belief that Wren himself designed the tower for a small fee. The nave is not particularly remarkable, apart from Thomas Swarbrick's fine organ case and the bread shelves on the south side from which loaves were given to the poor as a benefit of a local charity, but the lofty choir is magnificent, if rather dark at first appearance. Some ancillary buildings at the east end also survived the fire — a vestry, a vault where holy relics were once stored, and a chapter-house.

The tomb in front of the high altar is that of Thomas Beauchamp, who commanded the English army at the battle of Crecy and died of the plague in 1369. He and his wife lie in effigy with their hands linked. His grandson Richard has a far more elaborate memorial in the Beauchamp chapel, which is the church's particular glory.

No expense was spared to produce a worthy tribute to this hero of the Hundred Years War after his death in 1439; the finely-detailed effigy in gilded bronze lies on a marble slab, protected by a framework of hoops, also gilded. The tomb is rightly the centrepiece of the chapel, although there are other monuments. Ambrose, the least distinguished of the Dudleys, lies nearby, while Robert, Earl of Leicester, has a characteristically huge and vulgar memorial totally out of keeping with the medieval surroundings which have been restored with splendid effect.

A walk down Church Street into Jury Street provides another chance to look at the handsome main street, and in particular at the Courthouse, built in the 1720s as a meeting place for the Corporation. Its best feature is the ballroom on the first floor, once the social centre of the town. Turn left towards Eastgate, which nowadays forces the traffic to go round it. The Oken Almshouses face the busy junction to the right of the gate, and the big house immediately beyond it on the left was the birthplace of the poet Walter Savage Landor.

Smith Street, lined with pleasant small shops, leads down from Eastgate to a road junction, and a little further on St John's House stands back on the right. With free admission this is one of the best bargains Warwick has to offer. In itself it is a handsome building of the Jacobean period, but it also houses two very interesting museums; on the ground floor is an imaginative display of costume and social history exhibits while the first floor contains the museum of the Royal Warwickshire Regiment, with a superb collection of medals and fascinating mementoes of Lord Montgomery, the Regiment's most illustrious member.

The walk back to the starting point is by way of St Nicholas' Church Street, which has its own mixture of interesting architecture. It may not be possible to get into the church itself, but it is an

St Mary's Church
Mainly rebuilt in early eighteenth century, but outstanding feature is magnificent fifteenth-century Beauchamp Chapel.

The Castle
Claimed to be the finest medieval castle in England. State rooms (some with waxwork tableaux), Great Hall, Dungeons etc. Extensive ancillary buildings and grounds with their own attractions. Slightly commercialised but interesting.

Warwickshire Museum Market Place.
History of the county, geology, natural history.

St John's House Coten End.
Social and domestic history, crafts etc. Also houses regimental museum of Royal Warwickshire Regiment.

Doll Museum Oken's House, Castle Street.
Dolls, toys and nursery bygones.

Grand Union Canal
Famous lock staircase at Hatton.

Lord Leycester Hospital High Street at West Gate.
Very attractive range of timber-framed buildings, established as retired soldiers' home in 1571 and still serving that purpose. Non-residential parts open to public.

Court House Jury Street.
Handsome building of 1720s with notable ballroom.

Priory Park
Children's adventure playground.

St Nicholas Park
Riverside gardens, swimming pool, children's amusements etc.

St Mary's Lands The Racecourse.
Walking, picnics, golf centre.

Bridge End
Picturesque village suburb on south side of Avon bridge.

Hatton Craft Centre George's Farm, Hatton, 3 miles north-west of Warwick on A41.
Range of workshops in former farm buildings.

unusual example of a late eighteenth-century rebuild with an added Victorian chancel. St Nicholas Park is a good place to relax in after a tour of the town since it provides not only rest and refreshment for weary adults but an excellent children's playground.

Before leaving Warwick, anybody interested in industrial architecture should drive down Saltisford towards the racecourse to see Britain's most attractive gasworks, built in 1822. By continuing further on the A41 the famous staircase of locks on the Grand Union Canal at Hatton can be visited.

The A46 from Warwick to Stratford is a very dull road indeed, and the alternative A429 is infinitely preferable. It leaves the big roundabout on the south-west outskirts of Warwick and at once invites a detour to Sherbourne, a secluded village with a mid-Victorian church that has elaborate carving round the door and statuary on the tower and north wall. It was paid for by a member of the Ryland family of Sherbourne House, who also provided the village's estate houses and school.

The next village is Barford, and its old centre is found by taking the B4462 on the left. The church is rather severe Victorian but has some interesting features including a 'churching pew' at the back and a fourteenth-century effigy of a woman under the tower. Monuments to the Mills family in the chancel reveal that the Rev John was incumbent for forty-six years and the

*The Gatehouse,
Charlecote Park*

Charlecote Park

Rev Francis for fifty years. Just beyond the church is the beautifully proportioned old vicarage (now Glebe House) and then a row of four highly-individual cottages. In the first of these was born Barford's most distinguished son, Joseph Arch.

Arch's remarkable life-span started in the reign of George IV and ended after World War I. His early years were spent as an agricultural worker, but his experience as a Methodist preacher gave him a talent for public speaking. In 1872 he addressed a large meeting at nearby Wellesbourne, thus inspiring the first steps towards the formation of a farmworkers' trade union. The immediate result was a major strike in south Warwickshire that ended successfully, and in May 1872 Arch became President of the National Agricultural Labourers' Union. In 1885 he was returned as the first farm worker to enter Parliament, but after this his militancy evaporated and he ended his life in comparative obscurity in the cottage in which he was born. His grave can be seen in the churchyard.

2 miles after Barford, a minor road branches right for Charlecote, the home for centuries of the Lucy family. There is a quite unfounded story that Shakespeare's departure for London was the result of being caught poaching deer in the park here, and the legend has put the house firmly on the tourist map, although it needs no Shakespearian associations to make it an attraction. The visitors' car park is opposite the entrance, and the attractive setting of the house can be appreciated during the short walk through the deer park, which still supports a large herd. The building is often referred to as 'Tudor', but in fact the only surviving portion of the original 1550s house is the entrance porch; the remainder is the result of a discreet reconstruction in the early nineteenth century. The owner responsible for this was George Hammond Lucy, and it is his collector's taste that largely dominates the interior, which has been reconstructed to show the appearance of the principal rooms in mid-Victorian times. There is a wealth of pictures and furniture of fine pedigree, but the items that usually linger in the visitor's memory are the more eccentric pieces like a huge Venetian table, an ebony bed and the amazing sideboard in the dining room, constructed by Warwick craftsmen and intended as a present for Queen Victoria. The restored outbuildings, housing among other things a display of horse-drawn vehicles, complete an interesting visit.

The village associated with Charlecote is Hampton Lucy, reached by a lane that skirts the park and crosses the Avon on a cast-iron bridge made in Shropshire. Many of the former estate cottages here were erected in the early nieteenth century, and at the same time the old church was demolished to make way for the present decorative building by Thomas Rickman. The impressive height of the exterior is matched inside, and the spacious effect is enhanced by the lack of obstruction between nave and chancel. The east end was completed by the addition of a graceful apse by Sir George Gilbert Scott in 1858. Intricately-carved canopied stalls give richness to the chancel, and there is artistry too in the pews made of Charlecote elm. A charming old school building stands close to the church next to the less picturesque modern primary school.

A turning next to the Charlecote car park leads to Wellesbourne, which long ago outgrew its old nucleus (or rather nuclei because for centuries there was a settlement on each side of the river Dene). As you enter from the east there are signs of the old village around the church, which has an exceptionally good memorial brass to Sir Thomas le Straunge. At the end of the church lane there is a small group of pleasant estate cottages and a handsome Georgian house opposite the Shakespeare Car Centre. On the other side of the bridge is a village green with some attractive old houses and a memorial at the spot where Joseph Arch addressed his historic meeting.

From here the B4086 takes you through the expensive eastern outskirts of Stratford, across the river and into the town.

7 Stratford-on-Avon and the Warwickshire Countryside

It was Nikolaus Pevsner who said that in order to appreciate Stratford we should forget about Shakespeare. He meant, of course, that Stratford ought to be looked at as a very handsome market town in its own right, but there is the lingering question as to how much of old Stratford would be standing today if it were not for its famous associations and its early development as a tourist attraction.

It has become fashionable to dismiss the town as a tourist trap intent on selling trashy souvenirs to American visitors. This might have had some truth not so long ago, but nowadays you could walk the streets for quite a long time without knowing that you were in Shakespeare's birthplace. It is a lively and friendly town, proud of its own intrinsic appeal and making no blatant efforts to exploit the people who flock to it.

The town centre is very compact and a tour is not hard on the feet. Leaving the main car park and crossing the busy junction on the west side of Clopton bridge, involves negotiating heavy traffic, but this is left behind on entering the Bancroft Gardens, which always have a festive air in the summer. Start by walking on to the old tramway bridge, now a footpath but once the trackbed of an early nineteenth-century horse tramway between Stratford and Shipston-on-Stour (one of its trucks has been preserved at the near end of the bridge). From here there is a famous view down the Avon, dominated by the theatre with Holy Trinity church

Shakespeare's Memorial, Stratford-on-Avon

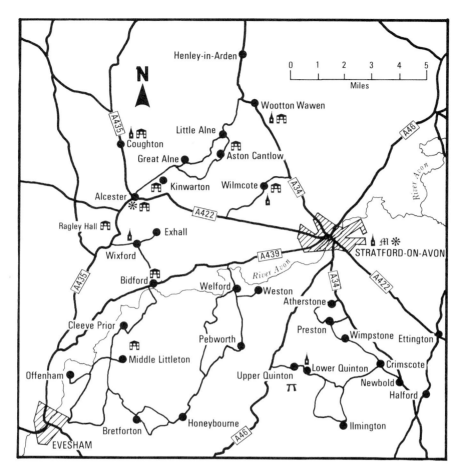

beyond. Nearby is the venerable Clopton bridge, the gift of Sir Hugh Clopton in the fifteenth century, which has been modified but still carries its traffic on fourteen sandstone arches.

One of the outstanding features of the Bancroft Gardens is the elaborate Shakespeare Monument showing the playwright seated on a plinth and guarded by Hamlet, Lady Macbeth, Falstaff and Prince Hal. It is a remarkably lively piece of work created by Ronald Sutherland Gower in the late 1880s. The Gardens were greatly enhanced in 1964 when the Stratford Canal was reopened after becoming derelict in Victorian times, and the basin here is usually busy with holiday craft that add to the cheerful atmosphere of the riverside.

Walk up to Waterside, the street that runs parallel to the river. Close to the junction with Bridge Street is 'The World of Shakespeare', a sound and light portrayal of Elizabethan England and one of Stratford's very few contrived attractions. There are some interesting buildings in Waterside, especially the terrace of low cottages after the junction with Sheep Street, but the Royal Shakespeare Theatre is the main focus of attention here. The first

Shakespeare Memorial Theatre was a rather intimidating Gothic structure erected in 1879; it was almost entirely destroyed by fire in 1926, but some idea of what it looked like can be obtained from the surviving portion next to the road where the theatre's museum and picture gallery are now housed. Elizabeth Scott's new theatre, opened in 1932, caused much dismay at first with its uncompromising brick and severe lines, but its inviting frontage and the imaginative use of glass on the river side, together with its green setting, have made it a very acceptable feature of the townscape.

Waterside becomes Southern Lane here. On the right the Black Swan now acknowledges on one side of its sign the nickname conferred by its actor customers over the years — the Dirty Duck. Further along is the unglamorous studio theatre used by the Royal Shakespeare Company for small-scale productions and known as The Other Place. Turn left at the end of the lane

and walk down to Holy Trinity church across the road.

The church is imposing — a reminder that well before Shakespeare's time Stratford enjoyed commercial prosperity as a market town and river port. The earliest foundation here in 1331 was a chantry chapel to Thomas à Becket and Henry V authorised a collegiate church in 1415. The nave is high and fairly severe in style, and the eye is drawn at once to the intricate organ case at the tower crossing. In the north aisle the small Clopton Chapel contains some medieval glass and dignified monuments in subdued colours.

If you now wish to move into the chancel you will find a barrier with a narrow gap, and only the most brazen of visitors will feel able to avoid paying the 'donation' requested. The attraction, of course, is Shakespeare's tomb and the memorial bust. Their privileged position in the chancel was the result not of his literary reputation but his considerable wealth when he retired here from

Shakespeare's Birthplace, Stratford-on-Avon

Shakespeare's Birthplace Henley Street.
Exhibits illustrating Shakespeare's life and work and the history of the house. Adjacent to visitor centre.

Hall's Croft Old Town.
Fine sixteenth-century house of Shakespeare's son-in-law, with period furniture and re-creation of Dr Hall's dispensary. Attractive walled garden.

New Place and Nash's House Chapel Street.
New Place is an Elizabethan garden on the foundations of Shakespeare's last home. Nash's House next door houses a small museum of local history.

Anne Hathaway's Cottage Shottery, 1 mile west of Stratford.
Interesting example of Tudor farmhouse that survived comparatively unaltered. Period furniture and bygones.

Mary Arden's House Wilmcote, 3 miles north-west of Stratford.
The home of Shakespeare's mother, a working farm well into the twentieth century and now a farm museum.

Shakespeare Centre Henley Street
Headquarters of the Shakespeare Birthplace Trust. Exhibitions held on ground floor.

Harvard House High Street.
House of 1596, home of mother of founder of Harvard University. Furniture, pictures, books.

Holy Trinity Church
Architecturally distinguished, contains Clopton Chapel, Shakespeare's tomb and wall memorial.

Arms and Armour Museum Sheep Street.
Interesting collection of civil and military weapons and armour.

Royal Shakespeare Theatre
Long summer season of Shakespeare performances. Adjacent Gallery houses theatrical pictures and mementoes, costumes etc. Theatre tours available.

Brass Rubbing Centre Avonbank Gardens, behind theatre.
Some famous Warwickshire brasses in replica.

The World of Shakespeare Waterside.
Multi-media presentation illustrating England in 1575. Frequent performances.

Stratford Motor Museum
Shakespeare Street.
Fine vintage cars, mainly 1920s and 1930s. Gift and book shop.

Charlecote Park 4 miles east of Stratford on B4088.
Original Elizabethan house largely rebuilt in early nineteenth century. Home of the Lucy family. Interesting pictures and furniture, kitchens and collection of carriages. Deer Park.

Stratford-on-Avon Canal
Southern terminal is in Bancroft Gardens. Good walk along towpath.

Dorsington Manor Gardens 2 miles south-east of Bidford-on-Avon (A439 from Stratford).
Home of Domestic Fowl Trust, with appropriate exhibits. Many other attractions in grounds, especially for children.

Welcombe Hills Nature Trail
$\frac{3}{4}$ mile east of Stratford on A46.

Shakespeare Memorial Theatre, Stratford-on-Avon

London. In fact neither tomb nor bust is particularly remarkable, but many visitors seem so transfixed that they fail to notice the fine windows or the misericords in the stalls. St Peter's Chapel to the south contains the unusual 'American Window', presented in 1896 by the American people; it shows various figures from American history in a portrayal of the Adoration of the Magi.

After leaving the church turn left into Old Town. There are some fine buildings along here, particularly the Georgian Old Town Place and the Croft School on the left, but the most famous is Hall's Croft, the home of Dr John Hall, who married Shakespeare's daughter Susannah. It is a substantial three-gabled house, well-restored by the Shakespeare Birthplace Trust, and the interior is furnished in Elizabethan and Jacobean style. The most intriguing feature is a re-creation of Hall's surgery, and visitors will also appreciate the immaculate garden.

At the top of Old Town turn right into Church Street, where there is much to admire. On the left the Birmingham University Shakespeare Institute occupies Mason's Croft, once the home of the novelist Marie Corelli, whose flamboyant behaviour enlivened and sometimes scandalised Stratford in the early years of the century. To the right is a magnificent range of fifteenth-century buildings comprising a group of almshouses and the original premises of the King Edward VI Grammar School, still an intergral part of the modern school. Shakespeare was educated here, probably in the schoolroom on the first floor of the building that eventually took over the town's Guildhall. The Chapel of the Guild is next door. It was restored at the expense of Hugh Clopton and is notable for the painting of the Last Judgement on the chancel arch.

Church Street becomes Chapel Street and the line of distinguished buildings continues with Nash's House on the right. It has an indirect connection with Shakespeare, in that Thomas Nash was the first husband of the playwright's grand-daughter; more importantly it is the way in to New Place, the site of

Shakespeare's own house during his retirement. It is now transformed into a charming Elizabethan garden. Nash's house itself contains a small museum relating to local history and there is a display of period furniture and household effects. On the other side of the road the Falcon Inn is a Tudor riot, but even more spectacular is the Shakespeare Hotel further along from Nash's House — it looks far too good to be true but most of it is authentic.

The wealth of timbering in Chapel Street throws the severe frontage of the Town Hall into sharp prominence. Constructed of Cotswold stone in 1767, it once accommodated an open cheese market at ground floor level, and on the first floor there is the customary ballroom designed as a meeting-place for local society. Sheep Street, one of Stratford's pleasantest thoroughfares, runs downhill from here and the harmonious buildings and interesting shops make a diversion tempting. Two features in Sheep Street of particular interest are the Arms and Armour Museum halfway down on the right and the establishment opposite called 'Abode' which has a charming courtyard.

From the Town Hall you finally move into the High Street, where the shops begin to monopolise the town centre. The rather showy timber-framed buildings on the left are the Garrick Inn and Harvard House, the latter being the home of Thomas Rogers, a butcher whose grandson founded Harvard University. The last house in the High Street (now the Information Centre) belonged to Thomas Quiney, the husband of Shakespeare's daughter Judith, and used to be the much-mocked Judith Shakespeare Tea rooms.

To get to Shakespeare's birthplace (isolated from the other famous buildings in the town) it is necessary to cross the road and walk up Henley Street. It is a workaday sort of road, and when you reach the celebrated house it turns out to be the least glamorous of

the Shakespeare properties: a model, in fact, of plain and authentic restoration with no prettifying. An attempt has been made inside to re-create the atmosphere in which Shakespeare grew up and there are displays illustrating his career. The vaguely neo-Tudor brick building next door is the Shakespeare Centre, where the educational work of the Shakespeare Birthplace Trust is carried out.

The short way back to the riverside and the car park is by way of Bridge Street, the broad and busy road that is bedecked during the summer with the world's flags. It has no famous buildings but its unstuffy, market-square atmosphere can come as a relief after the intense pursuit of history. Bridge Street can probably claim to have Britain's most elegant Marks and Spencer's as well as a half-timbered Woolworth's.

Stratford is an excellent centre for touring a large part of Warwickshire, and although a detailed description of the intricate countryside is impossible in a book of this scope the following four itineraries will include many of the small villages and market towns that give the county its character.

To begin with the area to the south, leave Stratford on the A34 and turn right after three miles for Atherstone. Almost at once the lane crosses the river Stour and the village is a short distance beyond. It is not much more than a small cluster of brick buildings and a farm, but the old centre is marked by the remains of a green and a huge, shapely chestnut tree. The church is dangerous and closed but there is a glimpse of a handsome old rectory beyond. In contrast to the commuterised country to the north this area has an unsmart 'working' air about it, an impression reinforced as you continue along the lane lined by unmanicured hedges with acres of cornfield beyond.

The lane turns through a sharp right angle and comes into Preston-on-Stour. This is an estate village of Alscot Park, the local 'big house', and it is one of the most attractive and least-spoilt places in

Warwickshire. On entering the village there is a timber-framed house leaning backwards in a novel manner, and then a fine village green where it is possible to park and climb up to the church.

James West, a mid-eighteenth-century squire, was responsible for having the church rebuilt by the famous Woodward brothers of Chipping Camden, although later restoration removed some of its Georgian character. The nave has a good Elizabethan roof with gilded roses, and the chancel is entered under a painted arch and through wrought-iron gates. The notable monument of 1624 to Nicholas Kempe and his two wives has no connection with the parish; it was brought here by West from a demolished chapel in London, and the same applies to much of the stained glass, which was accumulated from several countries. Note the modern memorial on the north wall of the nave, consisting of a bronze crucifix set on ancient timber.

After leaving the church walk down the village street between the two rows of trim nineteenth-century estate

cottages, and take the left turn towards the bottom which enables you to see the rest of the village. It is formed of unassuming houses in a mixture of styles, and mercifully no-one seems to mind the weeds and rambling hedges that that add character to this very pleasant place.

A mile from Preston the hamlet of Wimpstone marks the start of an isolated road with views down to the left over the valley of the Stour. Just outside Wimpstone, Whitchurch Farm lies beside the road as a reminder that there was once as village of that name to the south; its disappearance explains the solitary church standing in the fields only a short distance from the large settlement of Alderminster on the other side of the river. (The church can be reached by a footpath from the farm.) Alderminster spreads itself far and wide in the distance. It was once just another estate village but because of its convenient position on the A34 it has been heavily developed in recent years and not much will be missed by

Houses by Preston-on-Stour village green

bypassing it. At Crimscote, follow the sign for Newbold and join the A34 on its northern outskirts. It is a pleasant stopping place with a pub, a green and a variety of houses old and new.

A glance at the Ordnance Survey map will show that Halford, just to the east, is the starting-point of two promising walks. The first, to the south-east, passes through Idlicote and then traverses unpopulated countryside before reaching the very picturesque villages of Upper and Lower Brailes. The other goes in the opposite direction, skirting Ettington Park and continuing due north. Rather than follow it to its end, where it simply peters out, it is possible to make a circular walk by branching east at 151:255494, passing through the

Ettington and picking up the path behind the pub which joins the Fosse Way for the return to Halford.

At the southern edge of Newbold there is right turn for Ilmington, 3 miles away. Ilmington stands at the hub of a number of minor roads and was obviously a place of some importance before the main roads passed it by. It is large but very compact because of its horseshoe shape, and its mellow stone is a first indication that this is the fringe of the Cotswold country. If it has a centre it is a little green opposite the Howard Arms, a pub with a fine, plain frontage. The church is further towards the top of the village and very rewarding to visit. Norman work shows in the tower and in the two interior arches, and an odd feature are the two transepts. The north is fourteenth-century and the south is an almost exact copy carried out (very deceptively) in Victorian times. On the north wall of the chancel a memorial tablet to a former incumbent states that 'he performed the duties of his profession far short of his obligations'. Another unusual plaque in the south transept shows a bear-baiting scene.

Keen walkers who have been searching the horizon for hills will be glad to see the land rising behind Ilmington, and there is indeed some good walking country to the west. One possibility is to take the bridleway starting at 151:209425 through Nebsworth and on to Hidcote Manor. The return can be varied by branching on to the lane at 151:187426 and turning right after nearly a mile on to a path back to Ilmington. It is also rewarding to walk through Foxcote by way of the lane starting at 151:207424 and continue to the village of Ebrington. There are various routes back, but try the path at 151:184403 which takes you due north until you meet the lane mentioned in the first walk at 151:187426.

The itinerary continues on country lanes north to the Quintons. Lower Quinton is now dominated by the housing requirements of the big army depot at Long Marston, but if the village has lost its character, St Swithin's church is still notable for a fine Norman south arcade, a fourteenth-century statue of the Virgin in the Lady Chapel, a Norman font and a wall-painting in the south aisle. The unique feature of the church is a set of heraldic windows by Geoffrey Webb which includes a random collection of insects, butterflies and birds. Upper Quinton seems much more remote, with a scattering of houses round an immense village green. Meon Hill is immediately to the south; at 600ft it is modest, but in this flat landscape it is a real landmark. Not surprisingly there is an Iron Age camp on its summit, which can be reached on foot from Upper Quinton.

The return to Stratford is by way of the nearby A46 through rather featureless countryside with a large disused airfield on the left. It is worth stopping on the way back to visit Clifford Chambers. It is off the main road and can easily escape notice, but if you turn into its long street you find the attractive old village centre at the far end. The road is closed off by the manor house — a much-restored red brick mansion — but a footpath to the left of its gates leads to a watermill and fish hatchery beside the Stour. There are two very authentic, unrestored thatched cottages by the manor gates and a half-timbered rectory. The plain church has a filled-in Norman doorway in the north wall and two good Elizabethan brasses in the chancel, but the outstanding work is a very handsome coloured wall monument to Sir Henry Rainsford and his wife, showing the couple with their three children beneath, the youngest looking very long-suffering in swaddling clothes. From here it is 2 miles back to Stratford.

The second tour explores the villages to the south-west. Once again the route lies through 'working' countryside and extends to the horticultural area east of Evesham. Leave by the A439 (Evesham) road and turn left after 3 miles to Welford, which stands in a big loop of the Avon. As you enter the village between modern houses and immaculately-groomed gardens, it becomes clear that development and over-restoration has done its worst here, and unless you want to stop and admire the lofty maypole it is best to pass through and take the lane on the left to Weston. Here there are some unpretentious thatched cottages and an excellent small church where the huge windows show off the interior to advantage. The ancient doors, the panelled nave and the two fine brasses in the sanctuary repay a visit.

Return to Welford and take the left turn to Barton. The road follows the Avon and there is the first hint of

Coughton Court

---

orchard country to the south of the village. Barton is a small place with a harmonious grouping of cottages near a pub with the unusual name of 'The Cottage of Content', and a footpath leads down to a lock and weir. Just beyond the village you join the B4085 and pass the outskirts of Marlcliff, another hamlet backing on to the river and worth turning off for. A mile or so later is Cleeve Prior, the first village in Worcestershire and a place of considerable charm. It is possible to park just after the King's Arms and walk back to the entrance to the village to see the manor house. It may be thought that this is all there is to see, but Cleeve Prior is deceptively shaped, and by taking the footpath opposite the King's Arms and walking along the edge of the churchyard you arrive at the real centre — a triangular green with an ancient tree stump. It is flanked by the village hall and a row of attractive low cottages. the main street leads away from here and is

a model of success in absorbing new buildings into an old setting.

After Cleeve Prior the road runs along a hill above the Avon. For some time now the surrounding land has had a distinctive market-garden look, for this is 'grower's country'. It is not beautiful (intensively-cultivated land rarely is) but it is hard-working countryside and the preserve of the stoical group of people who opt for one of the most precarious ways of living off the land, constantly vulnerable to weather or political conditions.

The road bypasses North, Middle and South Littleton in quick succession. There is nothing picturesque about them, but one thing should certainly not be missed. Turn left into Middle Littleton and follow the lane down about half a mile to the church. At the back of it is an immense medieval barn, dating from abut 1300 and still in use, although now in the ownership of the National Trust and open to the public.

Guild Chapel and Almshouses, Stratford-on-Avon

136ft long and 36ft wide, it has massive roof timbers and two huge waggon porches.

Down by the river on the other side of the B4085 Offenham has become something of a resort for Midlanders, with a large caravan park, a popular pub and much fishing and boating activity. During the summer the scene is enhanced by the procession of holiday craft negotiating the lock. With Evesham virtually in sight, this is the furthest point of the itinerary, but walkers should note the possibilities of the path that leaves Offenham opposite the church, crosses the fields to meet the river at 150:066472 and then follows the bank to Marlcliff and then Bidford.

The run back to Stratford starts on the minor road through Offenham Cross and Blackminster. After 3½ miles it reaches Bretforton, a sprawling village these days but with a charming centre comprising a green, a manor house and The Fleece, which is believed to be the oldest pub in Worcestershire and one of very few village inns owned by the National Trust. Its great pride is a set of pewter ware given by Cromwell in exchange for the equivalent in silver. The church has been heavily restored, but one of the columns in the nave has a thirteenth-century capital illustrating the legend of St Margaret of Antioch, who used a crucifix to prise open the jaws of a dragon that had swallowed her. In the south chapel there is an exquisitely-carved medieval bench and the windows here have unusual landscaped scenes. The steps to the former rood loft have survived.

From the northern edge of Bretforton a lane leads to a place called Honeybourne on the map, although it is in fact two villages separated by the Roman Ryknield Street. Cow Honeybourne, to the west, is a nondescript place with a vestigial village green; a few yards from here, a rare example of a church converted to a private house can be found. Church Honeybourne is equally undistinguished, although its church, isolated on the southern outskirts, has some interesting architectural details, including a quaint stone-roofed porch and a massive buttress propping up the tower.

Return to the village street, pass under the railway and make for the more rewarding village of Pebworth, 2 miles away. The original centre is on a steep hill with the church occupying a commanding position. It has a fine medieval door and ironwork, but restoration has not left a great deal of interest apart from the remains of the rood-loft stairway and a very impressive eighteenth-century memorial to Robert Martin in the south aisle. Ranged about the church are large and small houses that have been restored in an unpretentious way. The three-storey New Pebworth House, its multi-gabled neighbour and the Knoll, a Jacobean house in the same row, are particularly handsome.

A rather lonely lane due north of Pebworth leads to Dorsington, where the Manor is becoming a very popular tourist attraction, and from there it is a short distance back to Welford and the main Stratford road.

In contrast to the last excursion into the fruit and vegetable country, the third of these tours is through familiar Warwickshire landscape, green wooded and prosperous looking. It starts on the A422 (Redditch) road, but after a mile or so turn left to find one of the world's most famous houses. Anne Hathaway's Cottage is in fact a fairly substantial farmhouse, and is one of the larger buildings in Shottery, which manages to retain the appearance of a village in spite of being almost engulfed by Stratford's housing developments. The car park is down a turning to the left as the village is entered.

Shakespeare's marriage to Anne Hathaway is shrouded in mystery, and we have no knowledge of what happened to her after her husband's departure for London, so it is interesting to discover that the descendants of her family occupied this house until 1892, when it was acquired by the Shakespeare Birthplace Trust. It is important as an authentic example of a yeoman's homestead, comparatively unaltered since the sixteenth century in spite of the chocolate-box quaintness inflicted on it, and its contents reflect its history and character.

After returning to the A422 there is a five-mile drive to Alcester, through pleasant rolling countryside. The main roads bypass the town centre and it is all too easy to overlook what is possibly the most attractive small town in the county. The car park can be found by driving to the top of the High Street and bearing left after the church; a footpath from it comes out near the church. It is best to begin by walking up to where the old Town Hall forms an island. It is basically of the seventeenth century, timber-framed above a stone-built ground floor which was originally open to provide space for a market. There is much to admire in this area. Henley Street, opposite the Town Hall, has some very distinguished buildings, the most unusual being the house next door to the Holly Bush Hotel, with its heavily pedimented first floor door giving on to a prominent balcony, but almost every house in this row is worth inspection.

Nearer the church, Henley Street leads into the narrow and intimate Butter Street; a little over-restored, although Castle House with its battlements provides an eccentric touch. The church itself was rebuilt in the eighteenth century, but its interior lacks the elegance usually associated with the period, and apart from one or two memorials there is little of interest. Note the clock positioned on the angle of the tower, presumably to make it visible from the High Street which stretches away handsomely from the church door.

Before starting to walk down it, cross Church Street to see Malt Mill Lane, a most successful example of conservation. The narrow thoroughfare is lined with houses restored judiciously to give a unified impression of a medieval street.

The High Street, like so many in the small towns of the Midlands, is a harmonious blend of styles with Georgian predominating. It is a pleasure to look at the countless interesting details of the façades. A few yards down on the right is a double-fronted shop with curious upthrust bow windows, while Bowen's, almost opposite, has very unusual sash windows, but the most elegant premises are those of Savory and Moore opposite the post office. The street is closed off at the bottom by the solid Georgian building that houses Lloyd's Bank. Leachfield Road runs along the side of the bank and as fine a row of modest houses as you will see anywhere, especially the former artisans' cottages towards the end. Considering the enormous development that Alcester has seen in recent years it is remarkable that its centre should remain so unspoilt while still serving its purpose as a very practical commercial area.

One or two interesting short trips can be made from here. A mile to the south-west of the town on the A435 is the entrance to Ragley Hall, the home of the Marquess of Hertford and well-established as one of the major stately homes open to the public. Less well-known is Coughton Court, two miles to the north on the Birmingham road. For centuries it was the home of the distinguished Throckmortons, who were originally a Worcestershire family (from the village of Throckmorton near Evesham) and who acquired Coughton Court by marriage in 1409. They are remembered mainly for their staunch Catholicism, but they touched English history at many points after the Reformation. A Throckmorton girl became the secret bride of Sir Walter Raleigh, and there was a Throckmorton

PLACES OF INTEREST AROUND ALCESTER

Coughton Court 2 miles north of Alcester on A435.
Home of Throckmorton family from 1409. Splendid early sixteenth century gatehouse. Fine furniture and pictures.

Ragley Hall 1 mile south of Alcester on A435.
Stately home of Seymour family, well-developed as tourist attraction. Imposing late seventeenth-century house with notable furniture, porcelain and paintings, including major contemporary mural by Graham Rust. Grounds by Capability Brown contain 'adventure wood' and amusements for children.

Ragley Hall Country Trail
In grounds of Ragley Hall.

Pleck Gardens North-west of Alcester, $\frac{1}{2}$ mile along B4090.
Wide range of flowers and shrubs, rare trees, pools.

Kinwarton Dovecote Off B4089, $1\frac{1}{2}$ miles from Alcester centre.
Fourteenth-century dovecote with well-preserved interior and original doorway. Key from Glebe Farm nearby.

Oversley Wood 1 mile north-east of Alcester.
Extensive woodland walks.

Great Alne Mill 2 miles north-east of Alcester on B4089.
Restored watermill open to public.

St Peter's Church, Wootton Wawen 5 miles north-east of Alcester on A34. Warwickshire's most interesting church, with substantial Saxon work and Lady Chapel packed with memorials.

plot against Elizabeth in 1583. During the conspiracy that became known as

Hoo Mill, near Alcester

Temple Grafton

121

Mary Arden's House,
near Stratford-on-Avon

the Gunpowder Plot the wives of some of those involved took refuge at Coughton to await the outcome.

The centrepiece of the Court is the magnificent Tudor gatehouse, and there are buildings of the same period at the back of the house. The remainder suffered damage first during the Civil War and later in 1688 when the Court was attacked by an anti-Catholic mob from Alcester. As a result, the wings on each side of the gatehouse are in plain Georgian style. In the house are displayed three items of particular interest: a cape embroidered by Katharine of Aragon; the chemise worn by Mary Queen of Scots on her execution; and the abdication letter of Edward VIII. Two churches stand close to each other beside the house. St Peter's is Coughton's parish church, and is noted for its stained glass and some fine tombs (one stands in an unusual position in the middle of the nave). The other is the Roman Catholic church and is not normally open.

Just outside Alcester on the B4089 is a right turn into a lane leading to Kinwarton, and this makes a very pleasant excursion. It consists of little more than an old rectory, a farm and a tiny church with fourteenth-century glass in its windows. A famous dovecot stands in the next field. Also dating from the fourteenth century, it has 600 nesting boxes and the original access ladder inside a low, ogee-shaped door. It is possible to take a short walk from here beside the river Alne to Hoo Mill, which is recorded in the Domesday Book, although the present buildings are of the early nineteenth century.

Another enjoyable walk can be started by crossing the river Alne by the bridge to the south-east of Alcester and taking the path at 150:086566. The track follows the course of the Roman Ryknild Street to Wixford, then turns east and climbs to the edge of Oversley Wood before descending to Exhall. The return is round the perimeter of Oversley Wood and back into Oversley Green. Oversley Wood itself provides opportunities for short strolls.

To continue the tour, leave Alcester on the A435 and after two miles turn left on to the B4085. The first village along here is Wixford, a small place with the usual collection of restored cottages and a church (down a sunken lane to the north) renowned for possessing one of the finest memorial brasses in Britain. Nearly five feet in length, it commemorates Sir Thomas de Cruwe and his wife and dates from 1411. Note also the wall brass to Rice Griffyn who died '3/4 old' in 1597. Outside there is a celebrated yew tree and a thatched shed once used by the incumbent to stable his horse. On driving out of the village you pass the Three Horseshoes, a very picturesque seventeenth-century pub, and 2 miles later reach Bidford-on-Avon.

High Street, Henley-in-Arden

Most guidebooks dismiss Bidford as hopelessly spoilt, and if you go there during a hot weekend in summer you can see why: the river banks by the old bridge attract a throng of families enjoying themselves in and out of the water. Few people seem to venture away from the river, but by turning just before the bridge into the narrow High Street and parking opposite the church, a most attractive little town centre with small Georgian houses and shops and several older buildings can be found. The High Street retains a good deal of character (it has one of Britain's prettiest police stations) and there is an interesting group of houses marooned at the far end where the bypass brutally cuts across. The venerable building at the corner of Church Street and High Street was once the Falcon Inn, reputed to have been patronised by Shakespeare. St Lawrence's church is spacious and dignified with a light nave and dim religious chancel; at its back the charming Grange Road leads away beside the river.

Return to the main road roundabout, take the Stratford road and turn left after half a mile for Temple Grafton and its neighbour Ardens Grafton. Their names make them sound snug and picturesque but surprisingly they turn out to be windswept hill villages with houses built of the limestone on which they stand. Ardens Grafton has a huddled air and is the more prettified of the two (there are exceptionally fine views to the north), while Temple Grafton retains more of the atmosphere of a working community.

Rejoin the Stratford road for just over a mile and turn left for Binton, where the church has a unique stained glass window. In the early years of the century the rector was Lloyd Harvey Bruce, whose sister married the explorer Captain Scott. After the deaths of Scott and his companions in Antarctica a memorial window was installed at the west end of the church. It shows four episodes of the expedition, including Oates' famous 'walk'. Another interesting feature is the mounting block with tethering ring at the gate.

Binton completes this itinerary and it now remains to explore the area to the north towards Henley-in-Arden. This is Birmingham commuter country, and there are very few places left unspoilt either by insensitive new housing, the over-restoration of old cottages or a combination of both. However, it is still possible to find features of interest, and the first stop is one of the more obvious. Leaving Stratford on the A44, turn left after 2½ miles for Wilmcote. Mary Arden's House is on the right just after the railway and canal have been crossed.

Mary Arden was Shakespeare's mother, and her former home is a splendid Tudor farmhouse with elaborate timbering and a tiled roof. The house and the farm buildings behind it were in use until 1930. The Shakespeare Birthplace Trust have now restored some of the appearance and atmosphere of Mary Arden's day, installing some fine examples of country furniture and creating a small agricultural museum in the farm buildings. Until the early years of the century, Wilmcote was a small settlement of quarry workers housed in rows of stone cottages — some are still visible though barely recognisable in many cases — and there was no church until the 1840s, when St Andrew's was built to embody the new ideas of the Oxford Movement regarding ritual and ornament. It is still a distinctive church, full of colour, with patterns and gilding in the chancel, illustrated texts on the walls, Stations of the Cross, sanctuary lamps and a very elaborate altar with a Tabernacle.

3½ miles further along the A34 the road passes under a canal aqueduct and enters Wootton Wawen (pronounced Worn), a village sliced in two by the widened main road. The river Alne runs parallel to the canal here, and drops over an impressive weir just beyond the aqueduct. The park on the right belongs to Wootton Hall, basically a seventeenth-century mansion and once the home of Mrs Fitzherbert, mistress of George IV. In the centre of the village the church stands on top of a rise with a green to separate it from the road.

St Peter's is one of Warwickshire's outstanding churches. Its castellated exterior gives it a late-medieval look, but

Norman doorway of St Nicholas' Church, Beaudesert, Henley-in-Arden

the bottom of the tower is Saxon work, and the heart of the church is still the 'Saxon Sanctuary' formed by the tower base, with its four tenth-century arches and some good modern stained glass. A medieval wooden screen gives access to the chancel, which has a fine fourteenth-century east window. Members of the Harewell family are commemorated here by two brasses and an alabaster memorial, and there are some rare fifteenth-century pews that survived Victorian restoration. On the south side of the chancel is a huge Lady Chapel — a riot of memorials that repay close inspection. Another rare feature of the church is the chained library in the south aisle, given by a seventeenth-century incumbent.

From outside the church the surviving buildings of the old village can be seen, spread out below. The Bull's Head is a rambling pub that has been 'improved' out of all recognition, but there could well be an interesting timber-framed building behind all the cheap embellishment. The same fate has overtaken most of the old cottages; carriage lanterns and imitation bow windows abound. There is a welcome touch of individuality in the red-brick house opposite the church topped with an incongruous thatched roof, and a good deal to be said for the Seymour almshouses next door, which have been built in sympathetic contemporary style and can claim to be the most pleasing buildings in the village.

Luckily nothing has been able to spoil the long sweep of main street at Henley-in-Arden, 2 miles further on. In style it is like Alcester on a larger scale, although less fortunate in that the main street is a busy trunk road. It would be easy to spend an hour here simply admiring the endless variety of the façades, many of them concealing much older buildings. While doing so, it is virtually compulsory to eat an ice-cream — the town is famous for its manufacture. The natural centre of the town is at the Guildhall halfway up the High Street, and there are some handsome buildings here. Severe restoration has left the church of St John the Baptist with little to show, but there is compensation if you walk a few hundred yards behind it and across the river. Standing on its own in surroundings that are suddenly rural, is the church of St Nicholas, where the superb Norman south door is matched inside by a dramatic chancel arch and small east window of the same period. The primitive air of this small church is most appealing. The hill behind it (accessible from the church) is the site of a Norman castle of which nothing now remains.

Return now to Wootton Wawen and turn right at the Bull's Head on to the B4089. After 2 miles take the lane on the left to Aston Cantlow, a village with strong Shakespearean connections — John Shakespeare married Mary Arden here in 1557. The name derives from the de Cantelupe family, one of whom was successively parish priest, Bishop of Hereford, Chancellor of England and St Thomas de Cantelupe. There is much modern housing before reaching the village centre, which is noted for one of the country's most distinguished parish halls, the timber-framed Guildhall that

was restored through the efforts of the residents. The nearby King's Head, and some of the surrounding buildings, are of the seventeenth century. Another fine piece of restoration is Glebe Farm at the south end of the village street where there is a right turn to rejoin the B4089.

It is a short distance to Great Alne, now a rather shapeless village with a couple of surprises. One is discovered up the narrow lane to the compact group of houses which marks the original nucleus of the village; a drive that used to belong to the Hall now leads to an enormous factory so well hidden as to be totally unexpected. The second surprise is the former railway station, best seen by continuing along the B4089 and turning left into the lane for Upton. Now converted into a residence, it is a flamboyant building with its original exterior features virtually intact. The church at Great Alne is a Victorian rebuild of a nondescript kind, but one other feature of interest here is the restored watermill to the south, reached by a lane from the centre of the village.

By continuing along the Upton lane mentioned earlier, you arrive at a rather confusing place called Haselor. In fact there appears to be no such village: the settlement consists of two hamlets called Upton and Walcot sharing a church situated between them. Parishioners experience a real test here because not only is the church on top of a hill, but access is only possible by foot. Both hamlets are worth looking at for the variety in their old buildings.

The lane that passes through Upton leads to the A422 and the return to Stratford, although after about 2 miles, a left turn leads to the remaining traces of the deserted medieval village of Billesley to the south and east of the church (a leaflet is normally available in Wilmcote church).

The second of these itineraries took in the countryside almost up to the outskirts of Evesham, and it is time now to look at the town itself and explore some of the countryside around it.

8 Evesham, Pershore and the Worcestershire Countryside

Certain placenames evoke clear mental pictures. We all think we know what Grimsby, Cheltenham or Scunthorpe look like even if we have never visited them. Evesham comes into this category, thanks to jam-jar labels and childhood geography lessons, but anyone expecting a sleepy town full of blossom will be disappointed. The town is businesslike, not particularly pretty, and has a serious traffic problem. Nevertheless it is worth seeking out its interesting features, and a good starting point is the Bell Tower, which stands on high ground above the river and is the principal landmark.

It is one of the few remnants of an abbey which was once vast in size and possessions, and could boast of a foundation dating back to 714. Abbot Lichfield was responsible for adding the tower in the early sixteenth century, only a few years before the Dissolution, and

no doubt it was its new-built solidity that saved it from the fate of the other monastic buildings, which were demolished and used as a source of building stone. What survives is an elaborately-decorated structure with ogee-shaped windows, ornamental castellation and much intricate carving.

From the foot of the tower there is a commanding view across the Avon. Evesham has made the most of its riverside land here, and the pleasant park and playground are a magnet for visitors in the summer, enjoying the holiday atmosphere of boats and water. The town lies on the opposite side of the tower through the former churchyard, where the sight of two substantial churches standing side by side may well cause some surprise. The explanation seems to be that St Lawrence's belonged to the abbey cemetery, and was later

The River Avon at Evesham

126

St Lawrence, Evesham

All Saints', Evesham

PLACES OF INTEREST IN AND AROUND
EVESHAM

Bell Tower
Only surviving remains of Evesham
Abbey. Tower dates from early
sixteenth century.

Almonry Museum Abbey Gate.
Exhibits illustrating history of
Evesham and district, including
agricultural items and domestic
bygones.

Abbey Park and Crown Meadow
Pleasant riverside park and picnic
area with children's playground.

Middle Littleton Tithe Barn Off
B4510 3½ miles north-west of
Evesham.
Magnificent manorial barn, fully
restored.

Annard Crafts and Woollen Mill
Church Lench, 5 miles north of
Evesham.
Mill open to the public, with shop.

The Fleece Inn Bretforton, 3 miles
east of Evesham on B4035.
600-years-old pub owned by National
Trust, remarkably unaltered.

used for the benefit of the many pilgrims who flocked to this important foundation, while All Saints' was the parish church.

St Lawrence's with the tower, is now redundant and locked. It is the less interesting of the two, having been given a comprehensive and fairly dull restoration during the 1830s. All Saints' also shows signs of Victorian attention, with a dark and heavy chancel behind a solid gated screen, but it has Norman work at the west end and a good chancel arch. The Chapel of Our Lady and St Egwin (c1513) in the south transept commemorates Abbot Lichfield who is buried beneath it, and there is some fine fan vaulting.

By turning right outside the church door you pass into the town centre through the Norman cemetery gate and along a picturesque passageway. It leads into a square almost closed off on the left by the old Town Hall, Elizabethan in origin with eighteenth-century additions. It once had the customary arrangement of an open ground floor for market purposes, but its arches have

been bricked up to provide draught-free accommodation. The medieval building that catches the eye straight ahead was formerly called the Booth Hall and is now known as the Round House, although it is demonstrably square. It houses Barclay's Bank and is an unfortunate example of excessive restoration, but it is a fortunate survival in view of Evesham's lack of major timber-framed buildings.

The Round House stands at the junction of three main streets. To the north is the High Street, a broad thoroughfare obviously intended to accommodate markets and fairs in the old days but now monopolised by buses and cars. The best buildings are on the left-hand side and range in age from the seventeenth to the twentieth century. Dresden House (1692) is outstanding; it acquired the name after an early owner, Dr William Baylies, became a physician to Frederick the Great of Prusssia and died at Dresden in 1787. Note also the Star Hotel, a handsome example of a Georgian inn.

To the east of the Round House is

Cropthorne, near Evesham

Aston Cantlow

Welford-on-Avon

Holly Bush House, Alcester

The rear of Coughton Court, near Alcester

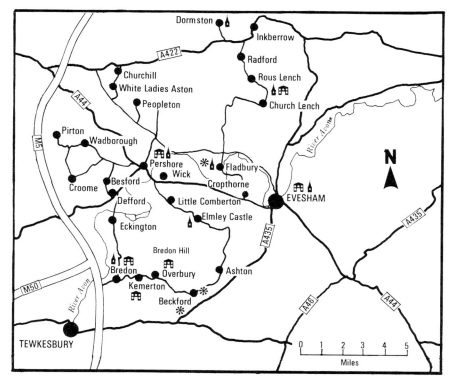

Map showing the area around Evesham, Pershore and Tewkesbury, with villages including Dormston, Inkberrow, Radford, Rous Lench, Church Lench, Churchill, White Ladies Aston, Peopleton, Pirton, Wadborough, Pershore, Wick, Fladbury, Cropthorne, Besford, Croome, Defford, Little Comberton, Elmley Castle, Eckington, Bredon Hill, Bredon, Overbury, Ashton, Kemerton, Beckford, and the towns Evesham and Tewkesbury. Roads shown include the A422, A44, M5, M50, A435, A46 and the River Avon.

Bridge Street, a narrow shopping centre that also has some interesting frontages remaining at first floor level. The mock-Tudor façade of Hind's the jewellers is full of character, but Bridge Street's oldest building is probably the Crown Hotel, a rambling inn now much altered and restored.

Finally Vine Street leads away to the south, with some distinguished buildings facing the Town Hall. They include the elegant Falconry Restaurant, the Royal Oak (brutally obscured, like Dresden House, by an enormous traffic sign) and a venerable pub on the corner of Vine Street and Merstow Green. The latter is really another square, and if you walk down the right hand side you pass the medieval grammar school which has now become a workingmen's club. It is worth continuing to the bottom to see some mellow cottages and the very pretty National Schools building of

1844, pink and mock-Elizabethan. Opposite the entrance to Merstow Green the Almonry Museum contains displays on local history and life; the restored half-timbered building has a front garden containing the town stocks and is flanked by some handsome Georgian houses.

From Evesham the Avon flows through giant meanders almost due west to Pershore. The countryside to the north of it is the heartland of Worcestershire, and the itinerary that follows is designed to include the most interesting villages, but do not be too disappointed if there seem to be few signs of traditional village life. In recent years the area has been considerably 'gentrified' with the result that the houses have been immaculately preserved but the old vitality of the villages has largely died. The general pattern has been that the people who would once have occupied the quaint cottages have moved (probably without much regret) to the enclaves of council houses on the outskirts, leaving newcomers to create the sort of environment that wins 'best-kept village' competitions. It is a pity that this reservation has to be made about so much of northern Worcestershire and Warwickshire, but it need not detract too much from the visual enjoyment of what is often regarded as quintessential rural England.

Leave Evesham by the 'new' Abbey Road bridge and turn right on to the A44. The road passes through the suburb of Hampton, and two miles from the outskirts there is a lane on the right leading to Cropthorne. The sloping village street is lined with restored houses, brick and timber-framed, and the church is right at the top end. It is unusual in that the main interest lies in the nave rather than the chancel. On the south side is a ninth-century cross decorated with birds and animals, while the north arcade shows traces of wall painting. The pews are distinctively carved. The most prominent features, however, are two coloured tombs of the seventeenth century; one is a table tomb and commemorates Francis Dingley who died in 1624, and the other, placed awkwardly askew against the chancel arch, dates from 1646 and shows the kneeling figures of Edward Dingley and his wife.

Fladbury lies a mile or so across the Jubilee Bridge. There used to be a traditional rivalry between the two villages, but the impartial outsider will probably find Fladbury the more appealing. It has a spacious air, with the time-honoured nucleus of church, green and pub, and there seems to be a lot of activity. The extra liveliness may be due to some new housing that has been absorbed into the village with unusual success. There is a wide range of older buildings, humble and stately, with mellow brick predominating over black and white, and one magnificent

Georgian house opposite the church. The best-known feature of Fladbury, however, is its mill, sympathetically restored as a private house and almost the first building passed as you enter from the south. Within living memory it provided the power to operate some of the first electric street lamps in any village in the country. The rather more functional buildings on the other side of the river are those of Cropthorne mill.

The Throckmorton family (mentioned earlier in connection with Coughton Court near Alcester) had their original home near Fladbury, and a family chantry was an early addition to the church, now a rather severe building with the neat and well-scrubbed look of Victorian restoration. The interest here is in embellishment rather than architecture; for example the small fourteenth-century glass panel at the Lady Chapel altar. It shows the Virgin and Child, and a specially-designed illuminated case allows you to appreciate the delicate colouring. There are some impressive memorials too; in particular the Throckmorton brasses on an altar tomb in the choir vestry, and two other fifteenth-century brasses, covered by carpets, on each side of the chancel. It is impossible to miss the marble monument of the Stuart period to Bishop William Lloyd that occupies the full height of a wall.

Follow Fladbury's village street to its junction with the B4084, drive straight over and take the next turning on the right to Church Lench. 'The Lenches' are a group of villages that must once have been very isolated; even today they have a remote air, with hills on one side and orchards on the other. Of the group Rous Lench is possibly the most interesting. From this direction it is entered by driving down a steep hill, and the first building on the right is Rous Lench Court, which is not open to the public but which has a gate that can usually be peeped through unobtrusively for a view of the celebrated gardens and of the house itself, which is a curious mixture of styles and periods.

The Court was the home of a remarkable Victorian squire and parson called Chafy, who ruled the village in a benevolent way between 1876 and 1916 and was responsible for refurbishing the church, thus ensuring its survival as one of the most remarkable in Worcestershire. The exterior looks entirely undistinguished apart from its small Norman door, but on stepping into the nave massive Norman pillars and a chancel arch of the same period can be seen. The staircase to the rood loft still remains, and there are two Elizabethan pulpits. On the north side of the chancel arch is a small mausoleum built by Dr Chafy and containing a variety of memorials removed here from elsewhere in the church. They include substantial effigies of Edward Rous and his wife (1611) and a rather quaint wall monument to Francis Rous, showing his wife sitting stolidly in a revealing dress and holding her heart. Another remarkable object here is a piece of carved stonework of Saxon origin. The church's biggest surprise, however, is the little Lady Chapel, Italian in style with a 'medieval' triptych, fluted columns, gold mosaic and an intricate altar canopy, all set within a miniature apse.

Rous Lench village is compact and charmingly set around a triangular

green, with remains of a roofed well and probably the only half-timbered post box in Britain. The unostentatious dwellings include a pretty converted school. It is all very dignified and contrasts strongly with Inkberrow, three miles to the north and reached by passing through Radford and joining the A422. There is a good deal of modern housing before reaching what is obviously the old village, where a lane to the right leads past the village green to the church.

Inkberrow is reputedly the model for Ambridge of *Archers* fame, and the Old Bull near the church does its best to live up to the image with much whimsical picturesqueness. The same applies to some of the other houses here, and the rash of new developments gives the place a suburban air that hardly justifies more than a brief stop.

There are, however, one or two worthwhile walks around Inkberrow. A good short stroll begins on the bridleway at 150:004573. It leads to Dormston, where the church has been less restored than most and still has a timber-framed tower with a spectacular array of supporting struts and beams inside. The nave has leaning walls, traces of wall painting, venerable sixteenth-century pews and oils lamps. At Moat Farm, further down the village lane, the Avoncroft Museum has restored a medieval dovecote.

A slightly longer walk from the centre of Inkberrow leads southwards to the isolated village of Abbots Morton. The return can be made by taking the path at 150:035553 and walking north to the lane at 150:032565.

A third possibility is a walk to the attractive village of Feckenham, to the north of Inkberrow. Start at the lane branching off a minor road at 150:013584 and turn on to a bridleway just past Morton Underhill. The path reaches the village by way of Beanhall Mill Farm and Grove Farm. An alternative route back to Morton Underhill begins at 150:015604.

Almonry Museum, Evesham

The village postbox, Rous Lench

Finally there is the Wychavon Way. This is a long-distance path links most of the villages mentioned in the tour so far. Begin, for example, at Flyford Flavell, three miles south-west of Inkberrow (150:982546) and follow its W symbol through Abberton, Rous Lench, Yeald Wood, Church Lench, Sheriffs Lench, Fladbury and Cropthorne. It is not specifically marked on the OS map, but it can be followed as a linked series of public footpaths.

Dormston Church, near Inkberrow

To the west of Inkberrow is a scattering of villages whose names could have been invented by P.G. Wodehouse: Upton Snodsbury, Flyford Flavell, Naunton Beauchamp, Broughton Hackett and North Piddle, to name only a few. They sound tempting, but being on or close to the main road they have become favourite dormitory villages and have largely lost their individual character. Very little will be missed by driving quickly along the A422 and taking the left turn just after Broughton Hackett to Churchill.

It was at Churchill that a group of nuns of the Order of the Poor Clares were given shelter after fleeing from the French Revolution in 1792, and they are commemorated by a tomb in the churchyard. A mile to the south, the straggling village of White Ladies Aston has some interesting houses and a church containing a memorial to a Victorian rector who served for the remarkable period of 71 years. Join the B4084, and turn left after 3 miles to reach Peopleton, a cheerful village brightened by the colourful gardens of the council houses which are allowed to line the main road here, along with expensive conversions. The church is a standard Victorian remodelling, but

there is a charming individual touch in a chancel window that shows a boy and girl unmistakeably of the 1930s.

From Peopleton it is a short distince to Pershore, where the first concern will be to find a parking place. Coming in from the north there is about a mile of 'suburb' before the A44, close to the town centre. Turn left at this junction into the main street and watch out for the inconspicuous signpost to the big central car park down a narrow lane on the left.

Pershore is a delightful place. The Avon loops round to the south and east but the town keeps a respectful distance from it; there is riverside activity here but none of the atmosphere of a riverside settlement. Broad Street, a square in everything but name, lies at the heart of the old town. At one end of it the long main street runs from north to south, its southern length a vista of harmonious and slightly aloof Georgian architecture and the northern stretch a concentration of commercial hustle and bustle. This rather class-conscious arrangement gives Pershore the advantage of having simultaneously a cheerful and convenient shopping centre and the most handsome and least-spoilt main street in Worcestershire.

Nowadays the town is associated mainly with the fruit and vegetable trade, but the original settlement grew up around a tenth-century Benedictine monastery. By an obscure process, most of the land here was acquired at an early date by Westminster Abbey, which led among other things to the building of St Andrew's church within a stone's throw of Pershore's own abbey. However, there are few relics of this early history in the streets now, and Pershore has a solid Georgian and Victorian character.

A walk round the town is best started at the southern end of the main street, here called Bridge Street. There can be few towns where the principal thoroughfare begins so abruptly; the transition from riverside meadows to urban street is instantaneous. Every house in Bridge Street is worth studying, and there is room here only to pick out some of the outstanding features.

Almost immediately on the left two semi-detached houses with lattice balconies make a pleasant change from the usual Georgian town house, but the characteristic style soon reasserts itself with the imposing double frontage of Stanhope House on the right. A little further along the same side is an interesting juxtaposition of two more double-fronted houses, both numbered 31 but originally two separate dwellings, one definitely grander than the other. The pub almost next to them has a curious tower and doors and windows that give it an almost Moorish look. Then comes Perrot House, once the home of a judge and revealing a very superior taste. Of impressive dimensions, it is notable for its Venetian windows; the central one on the first floor is conventionally flat, but on the ground floor the design has been adapted for bay windows. The front door echoes the window shapes. Back on the left hand side there is now an attractive range of small shopfronts, while opposite them Bedford House has canopied balconies of intricate ironwork.

The turning into Broad Street is monopolised by the Three Tuns Hotel, with a sheer north wall relieved by wrought-iron balconies. The spacious effect of Broad Street is diminished nowadays by the ranks of parked cars, but is remains one Pershore's best features, lined with small-scale shops and houses and closed off splendidly by a large house at the western end.

This is the way to the Abbey, which, with no disrespect intended, must be counted as something of an oddity. Although the monastic foundation was of pre-Conquest origin, the building that existed at the Dissolution was largely of the thirteenth century. As at Malvern and Tewkesbury, the people of Pershore tried to purchase the Abbey but were rather less fortunate than their

High Street, Pershore

neighbours; they were too late to prevent the nave being demolished and were left only with the tower, the transepts and the choir. This still represents a good deal of space, but the loss of the nave means that the tower has had to be buttressed in rather unsightly fashion and the truncated exterior lacks graceful proportions.

On entering the west door, the visitor is bound to be impressed by the superb arcades and vaulting, but will also notice the lack of an opulent east window. The Victorian love of a dim religious light in the sanctuary led to the building of a rather pokey apse for the high altar with minimal lancet windows. Bringing the altar forward has done something to produce a sense of space, but the east end remains claustrophobic, with the converging arcades adding to the funnel-like effect and concealing the two side chapels. In the south aisle, two large windows have Victorian glass depicting episodes in the history of the abbey in a series of small panels.

The west end, and in particular the south transept, has a pleasingly rugged

Pershore Abbey

air, with exposed stone blocks and big blind arches. An elaborate Stuart monument dominates one wall, and there are two much earlier tombs of an Abbot and a Knight Templar. The Elizabethan monument in the north transept is without its effigies, but the nine children of the couple commemorated are carved in relief on the front — eight of them earnestly praying and one of the girls apparently taking no interest at all in the proceedings. It is a rare experience to be able to see so much of the interior of the tower, where the unbroken view is made possible by a delicately-constructed bell-ringers' platform that makes a floor unnecessary.

The town walk is concluded by returning down Broad Street and turning left at the end into High Street. The buildings that face into Broad Street on the opposite side of the road are all distinguished, but none more so than the elegant Angel Inn with its four bow windows. By comparsion with the rest of the town, High Street seethes with activity, making a leisurely study of the architecture difficult. The main interest here lies in trying to guess the ages of the shops, since conversion, restoration and general 'doing up' has produced many bland façades that must conceal older interiors, the interesting group on the north corner of Church Street being a case in point.

From Pershore it is possible to tour some of the best of the Worcestershire countryside, the area that lies around Bredon Hill to the south. The hill itself is not dramatic by ordinary standards, being simply a sprawling expanse of higher ground, but in this flat countryside it takes on some significance.

Before starting it is worth visiting the small village of Wick, reached by taking the Evesham road and turning left shortly after Avon bridge. It is not a showpiece like some of its neighbours but an excellent example of how to integrate a variety of buildings of various ages into a single community. It is a foretaste of the unpretentious villages that can still be found in southern Worcestershire, where commuter pressure makes far less impact.

Return towards Pershore and take the minor road on the left before the bridge, following the signs for Little Comberton. The contrast between this shaggy, pastoral countryside and the manicured landscape further north is noticeable immediately. There is nothing remarkable at Little Comberton unless it is the line of headstones in the churchyard commemorating generations of the Yeend-Pitcher family, but it is a pleasant place which has absorbed its newer housing well. A few hundred yards on the other side of the village is the signposted start of one of the shorter paths to the top of Bredon Hill, and just beyond it on the left it is possible to catch a glimpse of Bricklehampton Hall, a Victorian mansion designed in an adventurous Italian style.

Elmley Castle can justly claim to be Worcestershire's prettiest village. The main street is generous and almost forms a central square, giving the place a natural focus that others lack. A stream runs down one side of the road beneath a row of trees, while on the right is a most interesting range of buildings, including the fine brick Manor Farm and an inspired piece of conversion next door. On a site that used to be a piggery, an E-shaped group of small houses has been constructed round a lawn, fitting admirably into its setting. The cottages next to it represent, quite by chance, the three building styles most commonly found in this area — timber-frame, Cotswold stone and mellow red brick — and the 'square' is closed off by a group of black and white cottages surrounding the Queen's Head. The handsome building opposite the pub is an old barn that until recently served as a village hall. A right turn at the pub brings you to the neat, purpose-built village shop and a splendid five-bay stone house.

Elmley Castle church is pure Cotswold on the outside, crenellated and built of venerable stone. Inside the porch look out for the carved pig and rabbit on the walls. The interior is rather dull, with the exception of some truncated medieval pews in the south aisle and several notable monuments. Of these the most eye-catching is certainly the blatant floor-to-ceiling memorial to the first Earl of Coventry. Apparently it was destined for the family church at Croome, but the second Earl refused to instal it there because he could not accept the pedigree which his stepmother had claimed for herself, and included on the monument. The unfortunate Countess managed to get it installed here when she married an Elmley Castle man. Infinitely more distinguished is the chest tomb of Giles Savage, who died in 1631. His effigy lies between those of his father and his wife, who is shown holding a young child. His four sons kneel at his feet. The tomb is a fine, crisp piece of sculpture, marvellously preserved.

An obscure-looking lane opposite the Queens Head leaves the village, and there follows a pleasant run across high, deserted farmland, surprisingly remote for these parts. The road eventually winds its way to Ashton-under-Hill, a long, straggling village that has grown a great deal in recent years. The old centre is at the southern end.

Beckford, two miles further on, invites a stop by providing a large and convenient parking place, outside the church gate. It is a highly individual

place, with a Victorian character promoted by an immense old rectory (now containing a silk-printer's workshop) and a number of harmonious estate cottages. The estate in question belonged to Beckford Hall, once the site of a priory and now once again a monastic community under the auspices of the Salesian Society. The south doorway of the church has been protected by a porch since the fifteenth century, and this has helped to preserve some crudely-executed Norman carving on the tympanum. The corresponding work on the north door, though of better workmanship, has suffered a good deal from the weather. The lofty nave retains its Norman walls and two original windows, and the twelfth-century arch at the central tower is finely decorated (note the odd carvings on the north column).

Half a mile out of Beckford on the Overbury road another path to the summit of the Hill is signposted, and it is about here that the invisible boundary of the Cotswolds is apparently crossed, because Overbury is very different from any village seen so far. Whereas Beckford has a casual, workaday air about it, Overbury has all the signs of being a rich man's hobby, and indeed it has belonged to the wealthy Holland-Martin family since the early eighteenth century. John Martin (of Martin's Bank)

came to live in the old manor house in 1723, and when it burned down in 1738 he built the present Overbury Court.

At this time the village was something of an industrial centre, with mills producing flour, paper and textiles, but in the late nineteenth century the industries died and some rather eccentric prettification began. The distinguished architect Norman Shaw was called in with instructions to produce instant rustic charm, and the results of his work (a little tongue-in-cheek sometimes) can be seen by walking up the lane to the north of the main road. A turning off the lane provides a vista of the Court's entrance gates and its pedimented façade, set off by some self-conscious cottages at the gate. A little further on is Shaw's superb village hall, and the lane goes on to give access to a mixture of estate cottages and more individual buildings, of which the best is Red House School, a lovely brick mansion with Venetian windows. Back at the main road is a regrettable mock Tudor post office, which might have some charm as a folly but hardly fits with the surrounding houses in traditional stone.

From Overbury it is a mere matter of yards to Kemerton, most of which lies off the main road to the north and south. It has an appealing centre with an inn and a house next door proclaiming Landaus, Wagonettes and Hunters for

Elmley Castle Church

Hire. There are no outstanding buildings here, but for the student of domestic architecture Kemerton provides a far greater variety of styles than one would think possible, and a walk along the village lanes is highly recommended.

Bredon gave its name to the Hill and fittingly it is the largest village on the tour. As you approach it from Kemerton, follow the signs for Tewkesbury, cross the railway bridge and then fork right into Church Street, where it is usually possible to park. The church is at the end of this road, distinguished by one of Worcestershire's few rural spires and graced by architecture representing all the best pre-Reformation styles.

There was a very early monastic foundation here, but the present building was begun in the 1180s by some very superior craftsmen. Their work can be seen immediately at the porch, which is spacious, vaulted and sophisticated in its decoration. The Norman work inside is confined to the short nave area and the western arch of the tower, different styles are apparent here; the two splayed windows facing each other in the nave

are in the early round-arch design, while the tower arch is later, with elaborate capitals and pointed apex. The big south aisle — the Mitton Chapel — is a thirteenth-century addition, notable for two fine windows (now distorted because of subsidence) and three recessed tombs below. It outstanding feature, however, is a vast marble and alabaster memorial to Sir Giles and Lady Reed, who both died in 1611. They lie in effigy under an architectual canopy with their children kneeling in small 'porches' on each side.

Major alterations took place in the early fourteenth century. The north aisle was added and a spire erected, but the most important development was the new chancel, where there is a canopied tomb of the period and an Easter Sepulchre that has had its crisp carving restored. Note also the decorated coffin lid and the set of heraldic tiles in the sanctuary.

Bredon village has a good deal to offer the visitor prepared to walk round. Just about every style and period of building is represented. In Church Street there are black and white houses of all shapes and sizes, together with the hybrid Fox and Hounds and a splendid Georgian town house. You also pass the backs of the Reed Almhouses, but these are better seen by walking to the fork at the main road and turning right. A little further on are some very expensive modern houses on which opinions will differ, and then a big milestone in obelisk form. Almost next to this is the entrance to Bredon's major attraction, the famous tithe barn.

In fact it was probably not a tithe barn but a storehouse for the crops of the large Bredon manor. It dates from about 1350, and is built on the same impressive scale as Littleton barn, about 130ft long and 40ft wide with nine bays and two waggon porches. There is a fascinating extra feature, though. It is possible to climb a set of stone steps to the Reeve's office, which has a projecting window to the front and a balcony on the inside to provide a commanding view of the whole barn. It was not a popular job,

and some inducement was provided in the form of a fireplace and a lavatory of simple construction — a hole in a window sill.

There is a short cut back to Church Street through the churchyard, but before leaving it is possible to glimpse two other substantial buildings near the church. To the north is the former rectory, largely Elizabethan, and to the west the stone manor house is a handsome example of Georgian work.

The return to Pershore is bound to be something of an anti-climax. Take the B4080 and very soon there is a right turn to Bredons Norton. There is not a great deal to say about it. Efficient Victorian restoration has left the church almost featureless, so that a modest memorial to Will Hancock and his wife stands out in startling relief. The village is very much of a mixture as before, with one depressing difference. The mellow brick cottage opposite the church gate and the restrained thatched house a little further

Elmley Castle

Overbury, near Bredon

up the hill show up the vulgarity of a huge and ostentatious modern bungalow on a prime site immediately opposite. In nearby villages, new development has been quietly absorbed, but here a single house has been allowed to dominate the view, entirely out of scale with its surroundings.

Two miles away, Eckington is another village sideways on to the road and consequently appearing smaller than it is. Double yellow lines discourage stopping, and it is probably better to continue to Eckington Bridge, where there is adequate parking space and a chance to relax by the river. The sandstone bridge is rightly famous, being the oldest on the Avon and longer than most packhorse bridges. The fact that it is half a mile from the village is a reminder of the lack of waterside settlements on this stretch of the Avon. The river meanders from Pershore to Bredon and only once skirts a village at

Greater Comberton.

After a mile the road joins the A4104, and a right turn lead back to Pershore through the nonedescript south-western suburbs.

The countryside to the west of Pershore makes a pleasant short excursion, beginning on the A4104 (Upton road) and continuing after 3 miles on the lane that leads off to the right after Defford bridge. The lane runs out of Defford to the north along the edge of a large area of common land which was once heavily forested and suffered the same fate as Malvern Chase.

After little more than a mile is the scattered village of Besford, situated down an even narrower lane. It has the only remaining timber-framed church in Worcestershire, a fourteenth-century structure with a Victorian chancel extension in stone, and the interior is notable for a rare surviving rood loft. Returning to the main lane and continuing northwards, from the roadside the mixture of buildings that makes up Besford Court, now a school, can be seen. Basically Tudor, the house was extended during the early years of the century by the celebrated architect Randall Wells.

At the next crossroads after the Court, turn left and after two miles watch out for a sharp right-angled turn and the impressive entrance to Croome Court, often confused with its neighbour because it was also a school until recently. Begun in 1751 for the sixth Earl of Coventry, its design seems to have been shared by several architects — Sanderson Miller, Robert Adam and even Capability Brown have all been suggested. Brown certainly laid out the gardens and possibly planned the nearby church as a carefully-sited feature. Past the gate, there is a short footpath on the left leading to the church, which is now redundant (a notice on the door gives the current arrangements for obtaining the key). The typically elegant Georgian interior contains some fascinating family tombs.

A further two miles along the lane is Pirton church, oddly isolated from its village and standing on a hill with a fine view of the Malverns. Its eye-catching feature is the Norman work in the nave (including the doors and ironwork) and a very early font surrounded by medieval tiles. The irregular windows in the chancel survived restoration. As at Dormston there is an intriguing array of timbers at the base of the tower.

The winding lane now passes through Wadborough and joins the A44 for the return to Pershore.

Further Information

HOUSES AND GARDENS OPEN TO THE PUBLIC

Acton Round Off A458, 4 miles west of Bridgnorth
Tel: 074631 203
Open: May-September, Thursday 2.30-5.30pm.

Ashleworth Court
Ashleworth, 5 miles north of Gloucester.
Tel: 045270 241
Open: by appointment only.

Ashleworth Manor
Ashleworth, 5 miles north of Gloucester
Tel: 045270 350
Open: by written appointment only.

Attingham Park (National Trust)
Atcham, 3 miles east of Shrewsbury
Tel: 074377 203
Open: April-September, Monday, Wednesday, Saturday, Sunday, and Bank Holidays, 2-6.30pm; October, weekends, 2-6pm.
Refreshments, shop

Benthall Hall (National Trust)
Broseley, Shropshire
Tel: 0952 882254
Open: Easter-September,(Closed Good Friday), Tuesday, Wednesday, Saturday, and Bank Holidays, 2-6pm.

Bishop Percy's House, Bridgnorth
Cartway
Tel: 07462 3298
Open: Monday-Friday, 9am-4pm and 6.30-9.30pm (also by appointment).

Broseley Hall
Church Street, Broseley, Shropshire
No telephone inquiries
Open: May-September, Thursday and Bank Holiday, 2.30-5pm (also by appointment).

Charlecote Park (National Trust)
Near Wellesbourne, Warwickshire
Tel: 0789 840277
Open: May-September, daily (except Monday and Thursday), 11am-6pm; April and October, Saturday, Sunday, Bank Holiday Monday and Tuesday after Easter 11am-5pm.
Refreshments, shop.

Clack's Farm
Off A449 at Boreley, Nr Ombersley, Worcestershire.
Tel: 0905 620250
Open: days vary each year; enquiry necessary.

Coughton Court (National Trust)
2 miles north of Alcester on A435
Tel: 078971 2435
Open: May-September, Wednesday-Sunday and Bank Holidays, 2-6pm; April and October, Saturday, Sunday, Bank Holiday Monday and Tuesday of week after Easter 2-5pm.
Refreshments, shop.

Croome Court
Severn Stoke, Nr Worcester
Tel: 090567 484
Open: daily, 9.30am-8.30pm.
Shop.

Dorsington Manor Gardens
2 miles south-west of Bidford-on-Avon, Warwicks
Tel: 0789 772442
Open: April-October, daily, 11.30am-6pm. Caravan and campsite, picnic area, shop.

Dudmaston Hall (National Trust)
3 miles south of Bridgnorth on A442
Tel: 0746 780866
Open: April-September, Wednesday and Sunday 2.30-6.30pm.
Refreshments, shop.

Frampton Court
Frampton-on-Severn, 4 miles south of
Gloucester off A38
Tel: 0452 740267
Open: by appointment.

Georgian House
7 Great George Street, Bristol
Tel: 0272 299771 (Extension 237)
Open: Monday-Saturday, 10am-1pm
and 2-5pm.

Greyfriars (National Trust)
Friar Street, Worcester
No telephone inquiries
Open: May-September, first Wednesday
in month, 2-6pm (or by written
appointment).

Hagley Hall
5 miles east of Kidderminster off A456
Tel: 0562 882408
Open: July and August, daily, 1.30-5pm;
Bank Holiday Sunday and Monday
1.30-5pm.

Hall's Croft
Old Town, Stratford-on-Avon
Tel: 0789 292107
Open: April-October, weekdays (except
Good Friday morning), 9am-6pm (5pm
in October),
Sunday 2-6pm; November-March,
weekdays (except Christmas Eve,
Christmas Day and Boxing Day), 9am-
4pm.

Hanbury Hall (National Trust)
Hanbury, 4 miles east of Droitwich
Tel: 052784 214
Open: May-September, Wednesday-
Sunday and Bank Holidays 2-6pm;
April and October, Saturday, Sunday,
Bank Holiday Monday and Tuesday, 2-
5pm.
Refreshments, shop.

Hartlebury Castle
Hartlebury, 3 miles south of
Kidderminster
Tel: 0299 250410
Open: Easter-September, first Sunday in
the month and Bank Holidays, 2-5pm.

Harvard House
High Street, Stratford-on-Avon

Tel: 0789 204507
Open: April-September, weekdays, 9am-
1pm and 2-6pm, Sundays, 2-6pm.
Winter opening times on application.

Harvington Hall
3 miles south-east of Kidderminster
Tel: 056283 267
Open: Easter-September, daily (except
Monday, Bank Holidays and Friday
after Bank Holidays), 11-30am-1pm and
2-6pm; February-Easter and October-
November, 2-6pm (or dusk).
Refreshments.

Kemerton Priory Gardens
Kemerton, Nr Bredon, Worcestershire
Tel: 038689 258
Open: May-September, Thursday,
occasional Sundays in summer, 2-7pm.

Lord Leycester Hospital
High Street, Warwick
Tel: 0926 491422
Open: weekdays (except Good Friday
and Christmas Day), 10am-5.30pm
(4pm in winter).
Refreshments.

Matson House
Off B4073, 2½ miles south-east of
Gloucester city centre
Tel: 0452 26572
Open: by appointment

Morville Hall (National Trust)
Morville, 3 miles north-west of
Bridgnorth
No telephone inquiries
Open: by written appointment only

Pleck Gardens
Alcester Heath, ½ mile from Alcester on
B4090
Tel: 0789 762553
Open: April-September, daily, 10am-
6pm

Ragley Hall
1 mile south of Alcester on A435
Tel: 0789 762090
Open: April-September, daily (except
Monday and Friday), 1.30-5.30pm, also
Bank Holidays.
The Park is open 11am-6pm, including
Mondays and Fridays in July and

August.
Refreshments, country trail.

Red Lodge
Park Row, Bristol
Tel: 0272 299771 (Extension 236)
Open: Monday-Saturday, 10am-1pm
and 2-5pm.

Shipton Hall
Shipton, on B4378 between Much
Wenlock and Craven Arms
Tel: 074636 225
Open: May-September, Thursday 2.30-
5.30pm, and Sunday in July and August,
also Bank Holidays (except Christmas
and New Year).

Spetchley Park
On A422, 3 miles from Worcester city
centre
Tel: 090565 213
Open: April-September, Monday-
Friday, 11am-5pm, Sunday, 2-6pm, also
Bank Holidays, 11am-6pm.
Refreshments.

Stoneleigh Abbey
Stoneleigh, 2 miles east of Kenilworth
Tel: 0926 52116
Open: because of Royal Showground
events opening times and dates vary,
refer to current literature.
Refreshments.

Upton Cresset Hall
Upton Cresset, 4 miles west of
Bridgnorth
Tel: 074631 307
Open: May-October, Thursday, 2-30-
5pm.

Westbury Court Garden (National Trust)
Westbury, 7 miles south-west of
Gloucester on A48
Tel: 045276 461
Open: May-September, Wednesday-
Sunday and Bank Holidays, 11am-6pm;
April and October, Saturday, Sunday
and Easter Monday, 11am-5pm.
Picnic area.

Witley Court (English Heritage)
Great Witley, Worcestershire
No telephone (grounds and church

only).
No fixed admission times.

Wilderhope Manor (National Trust)
Off B4371, 6 miles south-west of Much
Wenlock
Tel: 06943 363
Open: April-September, Wednesday and
Saturday, 2-6.30pm; October-March,
Saturday, 2-6.30pm.

CASTLES

Berkeley Castle
Off A38, 12 miles south of Gloucester
Tel: 0453 810332
Open: May-August, Tuesday-Saturday,
11am-5pm, Sunday, 2-5pm; April and
September, Tuesday-Sunday, 2-5pm;
October, Sunday,
2-4.30pm; also Bank Holidays, 11am-
5pm.
Refreshments.

Eastnor Castle
1½ miles south-east of Ledbury on A438
Tel: 0531 2304
Open: July and August, Wednesday,
Thursday, Sunday and Bank Holidays,
2.15-6pm; mid-May, June and
September, Sunday, 2.15-6pm.
Refreshments.

Kenilworth Castle (English Hertiage)
Kenilworth
Open: April, daily, 9.30am-5.30pm;
May-September, daily, 9.30am-7pm;
March and October, weekdays, 9.30am-
5.30pm, Sunday 2-6.30pm; November-
February, weekdays, 9.30am-4pm,
Sunday, 2-4pm.

Shrewsbury Castle
Castle Gates, Shrewsbury
Tel: 0743 52019
Open: Easter-September, daily, 10am-
7pm; October-Easter, Monday-
Saturday, 10am-4pm.

Warwick Castle
Tel: 0926 495421
Open: January and February, 10am-
4.30pm; March-October, 10am-5.30pm;

November and December, 10am-4.30pm
(closed Christmas Day).
Refreshments.

MUSEUMS

Almonry Museum
Abbey Gate, Evesham
Tel: 0386 6944
Open: Good Friday-end September,
Tuesday, Thursday, Friday, Saturday
and Bank Holidays, 10am-5pm,
Sundays, 2-5pm.

Anne Hathaway's Cottage
Shottery, Nr Stratford-on-Avon
Tel: 0789 292100
Open: April-October, weekdays, (except
Good Friday monring), 9am-6pm (5pm
in October), Sunday, 10am-6pm;
November-March, weekdays, (except
Christmas Eve, Christmas Day and
Boxing Day), 9am-4.30pm, Sunday 1.30-
4.30pm.

Arms and Armour Museum
Sheep Street, Stratford-on-Avon
Tel: 0789 293453
Open: April-October, 10am-6pm;
November-March, 10am-5pm.

Avoncroft Museum of Buildings
Stoke Heath (off A38, south of
Bromsgrove)
Tel: 0527 31886
Open: March-November, daily,(except
Monday in March and November),
10.30am-5.30pm (or dusk).
Car park, shop, refreshments, picnic
area.

Bewdley Museum
The Shambles, Load Street, Bewdley
Tel: 0299 403573
Open: March-November, weekdays,
10am-5.30pm; Sunday, 2-5.30pm.

Blaise Castle House
Henbury, Bristol (2 miles south of
junction 17 on M5)
Tel: 0272 506789
Open: Saturday-Wednesday, 10am-1pm
and 2-5pm.
Car park.

Bristol City Museum and Art Gallery
Queen's Road, Bristol
Tel: 0272 299771
Open: Monday-Saturday, 10am-5pm.
Shop, refreshments.

Bristol Industrial Museum
Prince's Wharf, Prince Street, Bristol
Tel: 0272 299771 (Extension 290)
Open: Saturday-Wednesday, 10am-1pm
and 2-5pm.
Car park.

Clive House Museum
College Hill, Shrewsbury
Tel: 0743 54811
Open: Monday, 12 noon-1pm and
2-6pm, Tuesday-Saturday, 10am-1pm
and 2-6pm (closes at 4.30pm November-
April).

Commandery
Sidbury, Worcester
Tel: 0905 355071
Open: Tuesday-Saturday, 10.30am-5pm,
Sunday also in April-September, 3-6pm
and Bank Holidays, 10.30am-5pm.
Refreshments.

Doll Museum
Oken's House, Warwick
Tel: 0926 495546
Open: daily, 10.30am-5pm.

Droitwich Heritage Centre
Heritage Way, Droitwich
Tel: 0905 774312
Open: Monday-Saturday, 10am-5pm.

Dyson-Perrins Museum
Severn Street, Worcester
Tel: 0905 23221
Open: April-September, Monday-
Saturday (except Bank Holidays), 10am-
1pm and 2-5pm.
Closed on Saturday for the rest of year.

Elgar's Birthplace
Lower Broadheath, Worcester
Tel: 090566 224 (pm only)
Open: May-September,daily (except
Wednesday), 1.30-6pm; October-April,
1.30-4.30pm.

Gloucester City Museum and Art Gallery
Brunswick Road, Gloucester
Tel: 0452 24131

Open: Monday-Saturday (except Bank Holidays), 10am-5pm.

Gloucester Folk Museum
Westgate Street, Gloucester
Tel: 0452 26467
Open: Monday-Saturday (except Bank Holidays), 10am-5pm.

Gloucester Regimental Museum
Custom House, Commercial Road, Gloucester
Tel: 0452 22682
Open: Monday-Friday, 10am-5pm (also occasional weekends and Bank Holidays).

Hereford and Worcester County Museum
Hartlebury Castle, 3 miles south of Kidderminster
Tel: 0299 250416
Open: March-October, Monday-Friday, 2-5pm, Sunday, 2-6pm.
Car park, picnic area.

Ironbridge Gorge Museum
On various sites in Ironbridge and Coalbrookdale
Tel: 095245 3522
Open: April-October, daily, 10am-6pm; November-March (except Christmas Day), 10am-5pm.
Car parks.

Jenner Museum
Church Lane, Berkeley, Gloucestershire
Tel: 0453 810631
Open: April-September, Tuesday-Sunday, 2.30-5.30pm; rest of year Bank Holidays only.

John Moore Museum
Church Street, Tewkesbury
Tel: 0684 297174
Open: Easter-October, Tuesday-Saturday, 10am-1pm and 2-5pm; some Sundays and Bank Holidays during the summer.

Kidderminster Art Gallery and Museum
Market Street, Kidderminster
Tel: 0562 66610
Open: Monday (except Bank Holidays), Tuesday, Thursday, Friday and Saturday, 11am-4pm.

Leamington Spa Art Gallery and Museum
Avenue Road, Leamington Spa
Tel: 0926 26559
Open: Monday-Saturday (except Good Friday, Christmas Day, Boxing Day and New Year's Day), 10am-12.45pm and 2-5pm, also Thursday evening, 6-8pm.

Little Museum
Church Street, Tewkesbury
Tel: 0684 297194
Open: Easter-October, Tuesday-Saturday and Bank Holidays, 10am-5pm.

Malvern Museum
Abbey Gateway, Malvern
Tel: 0464 67811
Open: March-October, Monday-Saturday, 10.30am-5pm, Sunday, 10.30am-4pm.

Maritime Heritage Centre (SS Great Britain)
Great Western Dock, off Cumberland Road, Bristol
Tel: 0272 20680
Open: May-September, daily, 10am-6pm; October-April, 10am-5pm.
Car park, shop.

Mary Arden's House
Wilmcote, Nr Stratford-on-Avon
Tel: 0789 293455
Open: April-October, weekdays, 9am-6pm, Sunday, 2-6pm (5pm in October); November-March, weekdays (except Bank Holidays), 9am-4pm.
Car park.

Midland Motor Museum
Stanmore Hall, Stourbridge Road, Bridgnorth
Tel: 07462 61671
Open: daily (except Christmas Day), 10am-6pm (or dusk).
Car park, refreshments, bird garden, grounds.

Much Wenlock Museum
High Street, Much Wenlock
Tel: 095285 679
Open: April-September, Monday-Saturday 10.30am-1pm and 2-5pm, Sunday, 2.30-5.30pm.

Nash's House (New Place)
Chapel Street, Stratford-on-Avon
Tel: 0789 292325
Open: April-October, weekdays (except
Good Friday), 9am-6pm (5pm in
October), Sunday
2-6pm; November-March, weekdays
(except Bank Holidays),9am-4pm.

Pack Age (Robert Opie Collection)
Albert Warehouse, Gloucester Docks,
Gloucester
Tel: 0452 32309
Open: daily (except Monday, Christmas
Day and Boxing Day), 10am-6pm.
Refreshments, shop, car park.

Radbrook Culinary Museum
Radbrook College, Shrewsbury
Tel: 0743 52686
Open: during College office hours.

RNLI Museum
Prince's Wharf, Bristol
Tel: 0272 213389
Open: April-September, weekdays,
10.30am-4.30pm, Sunday 11am-5pm.
Car park.

Rowley's House
Barker Street, Shrewsbury
Tel: 0743 61196
Open: Monday-Saturday, 10am-5pm

Royal Shakespeare Theatre Gallery
Waterside, Stratford-on-Avon
Tel: 0789 296655
Open: Monday-Saturday, 9am-6pm,
Sunday, 12 noon-5pm.

St John's House
Coten End, Warwick
Tel: 0926 493431 (Extension 2021)
Open: Tuesday-Saturday, 10am-
12.30pm and 1.30-5.30pm, also Sundays
in May-September 2.30-5pm.

St Nicholas' Church Museum
St Nicholas' Street, Bristol
Tel: 0272 299771 (Extension 243)
Open: Monday-Saturday, 10am-5pm.

Shakespeare's Birthplace
Henley Street, Stratford-on-Avon
Tel: 0789 204016
Open: April-October, weekdays(except

Good Friday morning), 9am-6pm (5pm
in October), Sunday, 10am-6pm;
November-March, weekdays (except
Christmas Eve, Christmas Day and
Boxing Day), 9am-4.30pm, Sunday 1.30-
4.30pm.

Shropshire Regimental Museum
Shrewsbury Castle, Shrewsbury
Tel: 0743 61196
Open: Easter-end September, Monday-
Saturday, 10am-5pm; October-Easter,
Monday-Saturday, 10am-4pm.

Stratford Motor Museum
Shakespeare Street, Stratford-on-Avon
Tel: 0789 69413
Open: April-October, 9.30am-6pm;
November-March (except Christmas
Day), 10am-4pm.
Gift and book shop

Tewkesbury Museum
64 Barton Street, Tewkesbury
Open: April-October, 10am-1pm and 2-
5pm.

Tudor House
Friar Street, Worcester
Tel: 0905 25371
Open: Monday, Tuesday, Wednesday,
Friday and Saturday (except Good
Friday, Christmas Eve, Christmas Day
and Boxing Day), 10.30am-5pm.

Warwickshire Museum
Market Place, Warwick
Tel: 0926 493431
Open: Monday-Saturday, 10am-5.30pm,
also Sundays in May-September, 2.30-
5pm.

White House
Aston Munslow
No telephone inquiries
Open: May-October, Wednesday,
Saturday and Bank Holidays, 11am-
5pm, also Thursday in July and August.

Worcester City Museum and Art Gallery
Foregate Street, Worcester
Tel: 0905 25371
Open: Monday-Wednesday and Friday
(except Good Friday, Christmas Eve,
Christmas Day and Boxing Day),
9.30am-6pm, Saturday, 9.30am-5pm.

CATHEDRALS AND CHURCHES

(Only churches of exceptional interest are noted)

Bristol: The Cathedral
 Lord Mayor's Chapel
 St Mary Redcliffe
 John Wesley's 'New Room'

Clifton: Roman Catholic Cathedral

Deerhurst, Gloucester: St Mary's
 Church
 Odda's Chapel (English Heritage)

Droitwich: Church of the Sacred
 Heart

Gloucester: The Cathedral

Great Witley, Worcester: St Michael's
Church

Leamington Spa: All Saints' Church

Malvern: The Priory

Pershore: The Abbey

Shrewsbury: St Chad's Church
 St Mary's Church

Tewkesbury: The Abbey
 The Old Baptist Chapel

Warwick: St Mary's Church

Wootton Wawen, Warwicks: St
 Peter's

Worcester: The Cathedral
 St Swithun's Church
 Countess of Huntingdon's Church

MONASTIC BUILDINGS

Blackfriars, Gloucester (English
Heritage)
Open: April-September, Monday-
Saturday, 9.30am-6.30pm, Sunday
2-6pm.

Buildwas Abbey (English Heritage)
Buildwas, off B4380 2½ miles west of
Ironbridge
Open: May-September, weekdays,
9.30am-7pm, Sunday, 2-7pm; March,
April and October, weekdays, 9.30am-
5.30pm, Sunday, 2-5pm; November-
February, weekdays, 9.30am-4pm,
Sunday, 2-4pm.

Kenilworth Abbey and Abbey Barn
Abbey Fields, Kenilworth
Open: June-September, Sunday, 2.15-
4.45pm

Little Malvern Priory
On A4104, 4 miles south of Great
Malvern
Tel: 06846 4580
Open: May-September, by appointment.

Much Wenlock Priory (English Heritage)
Open: May-September, weekdays,
9.30am-7pm, Sundays, 2-7pm; March,
April and October, weekdays, 9.30am-
5.30pm, Sunday, 2-5.30pm; November-
February, weekdays, 9.30am-4pm,
Sunday, 2-4pm.

ZOOS, WILDLIFE PARKS, WILDLIFE SANCTUARIES

Birtsmorton Waterfowl Sanctuary
Birtsmorton, off A438 7 miles west of
Tewkesbury
Tel: 068481 376
Open: daily (except Christmas Day),
11am-6pm.

Bristol Zoo
Clifton Down, Bristol
Tel: 0272 738951
Open: daily (except Christmas Day),
weekdays, 9am (Sunday 10am) to
5.30pm.

Butterfly World
Yockleton, on B4386 5 miles west of
Shrewsbury
Tel: 074384 217
Open: May-September, daily, 10am-
6pm.

Delamere Bird Garden
Fladbury, Evesham
Tel: 0386 860580
Open: daily, 10am-dusk.

Prinknash Bird Park
2 miles north of Painswick, Gloucester

on A46
Tel: 0452 812727
Open: Easter-October, 10am-6pm.

Southam Zoo
Daventry Road, Southam, Warwicks
Tel: 092681 2431
Open: daily, 10am-dusk.

West Midland Safari Park
On A456 between Bewdley and
Kidderminster
Tel: 0299 402114
Open: mid-March-end October, daily,
10am-5pm.

Wildfowl Trust
Slimbridge, off A38 12 miles south of
Gloucester
Tel: 045389 333
Open: daily, (except Christmas Day and
Boxing Day), 9.30am-5pm (or dusk).

RAILWAYS

Bridgnorth Cable Railway
A late Victorian funicular railway still in
regular use. It connects High Town with
Low Town, a distance of just over 200ft,
and has a gradient of 4 in 7.

Severn Valley Railway
The largest preserved steam railway
(standard gauge) in Britain. It runs for
12 miles between Bridgnorth and
Bewdley, and at the time of writing an
extension is planned to Kidderminster.
The termini are open all year, but train
services vary according to the season.
Detailed timetables are available at all
Information Centres in the region.

FACTORY VISITS

Berrow's Newspapers
Hylton Road, Worcester
Tel: 0905 423434
Open: Tours of printing plant on
Wednesdays at 5.30pm. Advance notice
necessary.

Brintons Ltd
Exchange Street, Kidderminster
Carpet factory. Tuesday, Wednesday,
Thursday between 2 and 4pm (not in
works holidays). Appointment
necessary.

Tomkinson's Carpet Factory
Duke Place, Kidderminster
Tel: 0562 745771
Open: Monday-Friday, 9am-12 noon
and 1-5pm, Saturday, 9am-12 noon.
Tours for parties of 8 or more.

Worcester Royal Porcelain Co Ltd
Severn Street, Worcester
Tel: 0905 23221/20727
Open: daily (except Bank Holidays),
9am-5pm; tours Monday-Friday by
appointment.

INDUSTRIAL ARCHAEOLOGY

Coleham Pumping Station
Longden Coleham, Shrewsbury
Tel: 0743 62947
Open: Whitsun-mid-September,
Tuesday-Sunday, 10am-5pm.

Fairbairn Steam Crane
Moored near Bristol Industrial Museum.

Grand Union Canal — Hatton Lock Staircase
Accessible by car or towpath, 3 miles
west of Warwick.

Hay Inclined Plane
Between Ironbridge and Coalport.
Upper end accessible from Blists Hill
Museum site, lower end can be reached
from canal towpath close to Coalport
China Works Museum.

Iron Bridge (English Heritage)
Freely accessible in the centre of
Ironbridge.

Stourport Canal Basins
Freely accessible.

BRASS RUBBING CENTRES

Bewdley
The Craft Centre, Lax Lane
Open: April-September, Tuesday-
Friday, 11am-4pm, Saturday, Sunday
and Bank Holidays, 2-5pm.

Bristol
St Nicholas' Church Museum
Tel: 0272 29971
Open: Monday-Saturday, 10am-5pm.

Gloucester
The Cathedral
Open: June-September, Monday-
Saturday, 10.30am-4.30pm.

Stratford-on-Avon
Royal Shakespeare Theatre Summer
House, Avonbank Gardens
Tel: 0789 297671
Open: all year, summer, 10am-6pm;
winter, 10am-4pm.

OTHER PLACES OF INTEREST

Albany Centre
Shaftesbury Avenue, Montpelier, Bristol
Tel: 0272 542154
Open times vary: telephone or see
current literature.

Arnolfini
Narrow Quay, Bristol
Tel: 0272 29991
Open: Tuesday-Saturday, 11am-8pm,
Sunday, 2-7pm.

Ashleworth Tithe Barn (National Trust)
Open: daily in daylight hours.

Bear Steps Hall
St Alkmund's Square, Shrewsbury
Tel: 0743 56511
Open: Monday-Saturday, 10am-1pm
and 2-5pm.

Bredon Tithe Barn (National Trust)
Bredon, near Tewkesbury
Open: normally during daylight hours.

Gloucester Antiques Centre
Severn Road, Gloucester
Tel: 0452 29716
Open: Monday-Friday, 9am-5pm,
Saturday, 9am-4.30pm, Sunday,
1-4.30pm.

Guildhall
The Square, Much Wenlock
Tel: 095285 679
Open: weekdays (except Wednesday and
first Thursday of month), 11am-
12.30pm and 2.30-5pm, Sunday, 2.30-
5pm.

Guildhall
High Street, Worcester
Tel; 0905 23471
Open: Monday-Friday (except Bank
Holidays), 9.30am-4pm.

House of the Tailor of Gloucester
9 College Court, Gloucester
Tel: 0452 422856
Open: Monday-Saturday, 9.30am-5pm.

Kinwarton Dovecote (National Trust)
Kinwarton, near Alcester
Open: during daylight hours (key from
Glebe Farm nearby).

Middle Littleton Tithe Barn (National
Trust)
$3\frac{1}{2}$ miles north-east of Evesham
Open: during daylight hours.

Moat Farm Dovecote (National Trust)
Dormston, $1\frac{1}{2}$ miles west of Inkberrow,
Worcestershire
Open: during daylight hours.

Old Baptist Chapel
Church Street, Tewkesbury
Open: daily (except Christmas
Day),9am-dusk.

Prinknash Abbey
On A46 3 miles north of Painswick,
Gloucester
Tel: 0452 812239
Open: Church, daily, 5am-8.30pm;
Pottery, Monday-Saturday, 10.30am-

5pm, Sunday 2-5pm.
Shop, daily, 9am-6pm.
Restaurant.

Royal Shakespeare Theatre
Stratford-on-Avon
Box Office
Tel: 0789 295 623

Watershed Arts Centre
Canons Road, Bristol
Tel: 0272 276444
Open: Monday-Thursday, 10am-
10.30pm, Friday and Saturday,
10am-11pm.

Wichenford Dovecote (National Trust)
Off B4204, $4\frac{1}{2}$ miles north-west of
Worcester
Open: during daylight hours.

World of Shakespeare
Waterside, Stratford-on-Avon
Tel: 0789 69190
Open: July-September, 9.30am-8.30pm;
October-June, 10am-5pm.

ARCHAEOLOGICAL SITES

East Gate
Eastgate Street, Gloucester
Tel: 0452 24131
Open: May-September, Wednesday and
Friday, 2-5pm, Saturday, 10am-12 noon
and 2-5pm.

Kings Weston Roman Villa
Long Cross, Lawrence Weston, Bristol
Tel: 0272 299771
Open: Saturday-Wednesday, 8.30am-
5pm.

Viroconium (Roman Town) (English
Heritage)
Wroxeter, 2 miles east of Shrewsbury off
B4380
Open: May-September, daily, 9.30am-
7pm; March and October, Saturday,
9.30am-5.30pm, Sunday, 2-5.30pm;
April, daily, 9.30am-5.30; November-
February, weekdays, 9.30am-4pm,
Sunday, 2-4pm.

COUNTRY PARKS AND NATURE RESERVES

Avon Gorge Nature Reserve
Leigh Woods, north of Clifton
Suspension Bridge, Bristol
Entrance off A369 $\frac{3}{4}$ mile east of Abbots
Leigh

Ashton Court Estate
South of Clifton Suspension Bridge,
Bristol.

Crackley Wood
1 mile north of Kenilworth.

Hartlebury Common
On A4025, $\frac{1}{2}$ mile south-east of
Stourport.

Newbold Comyn
Eastern outskirts of Leamington Spa.

Nunnery Wood Country Park
Spetchley Road, Worcester (adjacent to
County Hall).

Old Hills
Callow End, on B4424, $2\frac{1}{2}$ miles south
of Powick, near Worcester.

Oversley Wood
Off A422, south of Alcester.

Ragley Hall Park
Ragley Hall, on A435 1 mile south of
Alcester
Open: April-September, 11am-6pm
(closed Monday and Friday except in
July).

Ravenshill Woodland Reserve
1 mile north-west of Alfrick, Worcester
Open: March-October only.

Robinswood Hill Country Park
3 miles south of Gloucester, between M5
and A4173.

Welcombe Hills
$\frac{3}{4}$ mile east of Stratford-on-Avon on
A46.

Wyre Forest
3 miles west of Bewdley on A456
Visitor Centre open: March-October,
Saturday, Sunday, Bank Holidays, 1-
5pm (also Tuesday-Thursday in
August).

CRAFT WORKSHOPS OPEN TO THE PUBLIC

(Open during normal working hours
unless otherwise stated)

Annards Crafts and Woollen Mill
Handgate Farm, Church Lench,
Worcestershire
Tel: 0386 870270

Beckford Silk
Old Vicarage, Beckford, near Bredon
Tel: 0386 881507

Clevedon Craft Centre
Newhouse Farm, Moor Lane, Clevedon,
near Bristol

England's Mills
Sea Mills, Berkeley, Gloucestershire
Tel: 0453 811150
(Stoneground flour)

Great Alne Mill
Great Alne, on B4089, $2\frac{1}{2}$ miles east of
Alcester
Restored watermill grinding flour.

Ironbridge Craft Centre
Old Police Station, Ironbridge
Tel: 0952 505051

Jinney Ring Craft Centre
On B4091 at Hanbury, Worcester
Tel: 0926 272
Open: April-Christmas, Wednesday-
Saturday, 10.30am-5pm,. Sunday,
2-5.30pm; January-end March,
Wednesday-Saturday, 10.30am-5pm,
Sunday, 2-5.30pm.

Lax Lane Craft Centre
Lax Lane, Bewdley

Midsummer Weavers
Old Drill Hall, London Lane, Upton-
on-Severn
Tel: 06846 3503
Open: daily (except Sunday and
Monday).

Hatton Craft Centre
George's Farm, Hatton, near Warwick

LONG-DISTANCE FOOTPATHS

Avon Walkway
This path begins at Pill, close to the
mouth of the Gloucestershire Avon and
follows the river closely through Bristol
and into Bath. The length of this stretch
is approximately twenty miles, and it can
be continued into Wiltshire.

Stratford-on-Avon Canal
Not a designated walk, but the towpath
can be followed from the centre of
Stratford through pleasant countryside
to Kingswood Junction at Lapworth,
twelve miles to the north.

Grand Union Canal
The towpath can be followed
indefinitely, but the most interesting
stretch is probably from Leamington
Spa, through Warwick and on towards
Birmingham, passing some interesting
features including the famous lock
staircase at Hatton.

Wychavon Way
A waymarked walk from Holt Fleet, 6
miles north of Worcester, to
Winchcombe in Gloucestershire, over
Bredon Hill and into the northern
Cotswolds. Total length forty miles.
Conveniently, the whole walk is on OS
sheet 150.

SWIMMING POOLS

Bristol
Bishopswood Pool
Whitchurch Road
Tel: 0272 640258

Clifton Open-Air Pool
Oakfield Place
Tel: 0272 737538

Filwood Pool
Filwood Broadway
Tel: 0272 662823

Jubilee Pool
Jubilee Road
Tel: 0272 777900

Evesham
Davies Road
Tel: 0386 47542

Gloucester
Station Road
Tel: 0452 36498

Leamington Spa
Pump Room
Tel: 0926 21251

Pershore
Avon Valley Pool
Tel: 0386 552346

Shrewsbury
Priory Road
Tel: 0743 3583

Tewkesbury
Oldbury Road
Tel: 0684 293740

Warwick
St Nicholas Park Open-Air Pool
Tel: 0926 45353

Worcester
Citizens' Pool
Weir Lane
Tel: 0905 421089

Sansome Walk
Tel: 0905 20241

GOLF COURSES

Most of the courses in the region are
private, and it will be necessary to make
preliminary inquiries about temporary
membership or daily facilities.

Bristol

Filton Golf Club
north Bristol
Tel: 0272 694169

Henbury Golf Club
Henbury, north-west Bristol
Tel: 0272 500044

Mangotsfield Golf Club
Mangotsfield, north-east Bristol
Tel: 0272 565501

Droitwich

Droitwich Golf and Country Club
Ford Lane, Droitwich
Tel: 0905 774344

Evesham

Evesham Golf Club
Fladbury, near Evesham
Tel: 0386 860395

Gloucester

Cleeve Hill Municipal Course
Cleeve Hill, Gloucester
Tel: 024267 2025

Gloucester Hotel and Country Club
Matson Lane, Gloucester
Tel: 0452 25653

Kenilworth

Kenilworth Golf Club
Crew Lane, Kenilworth
Tel: 0926 54296

Kidderminster

Kidderminster Golf club
Russell Road, Kidderminster
Tel: 0562 2303

Leamington Spa

Municipal Golf Course
Newbold Comyn, Leamington Spa
Tel: 0926 21157

Leamington and County Golf Club
Tel: 0926 25961

Malvern

Worcestershire Golf Club
Malvern
Tel: 06845 5992

Shrewsbury

Shrewsbury Golf Club
Condover
Tel: 074372 2977

Municipal Course
Meole Brace
Tel: 0743 64050

Stratford-on-Avon

Stratford Golf Club
Tiddington Road, Stratford-on-Avon
Tel: 0789 205749

Tewkesbury

Tewkesbury Park Hotel, Golf and Country Club
Lincoln Green Lane, Tewkesbury
Tel: 0684 295405

Warwick

Warwick Golf Centre
Racecourse, Warwick
Tel: 0926 494316

Worcester

Tolladine Golf Club
Tolladine Road, Worcester
Tel: 0905 21074

Worcester Golf Range
Weir Lane, Worcester
Tel: 0905 421213

RIDING STABLES

Alderminster, Warwicks

Ettington Park Riding Stables
Alderminster, Warwickshire
Tel: 078987 653

Bristol

Gordano Valley Riding Club
Clapton-in-Gordano, Portishead,
Bristol
Tel: 0272 843473

Gloucester

Huntley School of Equitation
Woodend Farm, Huntley
Tel: 0466 830440

Moorend Riding Centre
Bullen Manor Farm, Upton St Leonards
Tel: 0452 66611

Ironbridge

H. C. Gittins
Rough Park, Madeley
Tel: 0952 585108

Kidderminster

Hartlebury Stables
Worseley Manor, Hartlebury
Tel: 0299 250710

Leamington Spa

Waverley Riding School
Coventry Road, Cubbington, near
Leamington Spa
Tel: 0926 22876

Malvern

Runnings Park Riding Stables
Croft Bank, West Malvern
Tel: 06845 65290

Shrewsbury

Prescott Riding Centre
Prescott Farm, Baschurch,
Tel: 0939 260712

Stourport

Rockmoor Stables
Rock,
Tel: 029922 556

Stratford-on-Avon

Pathlow Riding Centre
Featherbed Lane, Pathlow
Tel: 0789 292451

Warwick

Warwick School of Riding
Guys Cliffe, Coventry Road, Warwick
Tel: 0926 494313

Worcester

Moorlands Riding Centre
Hindlip Lane, Worcester
Tel: 0905 51487

RIVER CRUISING AND BOAT HIRE

Bristol

Bristol and Bath Cruisers
Lower Guinea Street
Tel: 0272 214307

Bristol Narrowboats
Bathurst Basin
Tel: 0272 28157

Droitwich

Brook Line, Trench Lane,
Dunhampstead
Tel: 0905 773889

Evesham

Avon Vale Cruisers
Common Road
Tel: 0386 2759
Small boat hire at riverside gardens.

Gloucester

Cotswold Narrow Boats
Frenchay Bakers Quay, Merchants
Road
Tel: 0452 29317

Stourport

Severn Steamboat Company (river trips)
Engine Lane
Tel: 02993 71177

Stroudwater Cruisers
Engine Lane
Tel: 02993 77222
Small boat hire at riverside park.

Stratford-on-Avon

Stratford Marine
Clopton Bridge
Tel: 0789 69669

G.H. Rose
(small boat hire)
Clopton Bridge
Tel: 0789 67073
Steamer trips from Bancroft Gardens.

Tewkesbury

Tewkesbury Marina
Bredon Road
Tel: 0684 293737

King John Holiday Cruisers
Bredon Road
Tel: 0684 292981

Telestar Pleasure Cruisers
185 Queens Road
Tel: 0684 294088

Upton-on-Severn

Upton-on-Severn Marina
East Waterside
Tel: 06846 3111
(Various hire firms)

Warwick

Kate Boats
Nelson Lane
Tel: 0926 492968

Worcester

Pitchcroft Boating Station
Waterworks Road
Tel: 0905 27949

BUS SERVICES

(The following inquiry offices will
normally advise where services are
supplemented by private operators)

Crosville Motor Services
(North-west Shropshire)
Tel: 0691 652402

Midland Red
(Other Shropshire areas)
Tel: 0743 3285

Midland Red
(Leamington, Warwick, Stratford areas)
Tel: 0926 22593
Tel: 0789 204181 for Stratford

Midland Red
(Worcester, Kidderminster, Bewdley,
Stourport, Droitwich areas)
Tel: 0905 23296

**Cheltenham and Gloucester Omnibus
Company**
Tel: 0452 27516

Bristol Omnibus Company
(City and rural services)
Tel: 0272 553231

TOURIST INFORMATION CENTRES

* Operates bed booking service

Bewdley: The Library, Load Street
Tel: 0299 403303

Bridgnorth: The Library, Listley Street
Tel: 07462 3358

*Bristol: Colston House, Colston Street
Tel: 0272 293891

*Droitwich: Heritage Centre, Heritage
Way
Tel: 0905 774312

Evesham (summer only): Almonry
Museum, Abbey Gate
Tel: 0386 6944

*Gloucester: 6 College Street
Tel: 0452 421188

*Ironbridge (summer only): Iron Bridge
Tollhouse
Tel: 0952 882753

Kenilworth: The Library, Smalley Place
Tel: 0926 52595

Kidderminster: The Library, Market
Street
Tel: 0562 752832

*Leamington Spa: Jephson Lodge, The
Parade
Tel: 0926 311470

*Malvern: Winter Gardens, Grange
Road
Tel: 06845 2700

*Pershore: Council Offices, 37 High
Street
Tel: 0386 554711

*Shrewsbury: The Square
Tel: 0743 52019

Stourport: The Library, County
Buildings
Tel: 02993 2866

*Stratford-on-Avon: 1 High Street
Tel: 0789 293127

*Tewkesbury (summer only): 64 Barton
Street
Tel: 0684 295027

*Upton-on-Severn (summer only)
Church Street
Tel: 06845 2700

Warwick: The Court House, Jury Street
Tel: 0926 492212

*Worcester: Guildhall, High Street
Tel: 0905 32471

YOUTH HOSTELS

Shrewsbury
The Woodlands, Abbey Foregate
Tel: 0743 56397

Ironbridge
Coalbrookdale Institute, Coalbrookdale
Tel: 095245 3278

Wilderhope Manor
Easthope, Much Wenlock
Tel: 06943 363

Malvern
18 Peachfield Road, Malvern Wells
Tel: 06845 3300

Slimbridge
Shepherd's Patch, Slimbridge,
Gloucestershire
Tel: 045389 275

Bristol
Late July-late August only:
St John Reade Hall of Residence,
Redland Green, Bristol
Nearest all-year: Bathwick Hill, Bath
Tel: 0225 65674

Stratford-on-Avon
Hemmingford House, Alveston
Tel: 0789 297093

Bridges
Bridges, Ratlinghope, Shrewsbury
Tel: 058861 656

Duntisbourne Abbots
Duntisbourne Abbots, Cirencester
Tel: 028582 346

Cleeve Hill
Rock House, Cleeve Hill, Cheltenham
Tel: 024267 2065

Useful Addresses

English Heritage,
Bridge House,
Sion Place,
Clifton,
Bristol BS8 4XA
Tel: 0272 734472

English Tourist Board,
Thames Tower, Blacks Road,
Hammersmith, London W6 9EL
Tel: 01 846 9000

Heart of England Tourist Board,
PO Box 15,
Worcester
Tel: 0905 29511

West Country Tourist Board,
37 Southernhay East,
Exeter, Devon
Tel: 0392 76351

Severn Trent Water Authority:
River Avon,
Avon House,
de Montfort Way,
Coventry
Tel: 0203 416510
River Severn,
Southwick Park, Gloucester Road,
Tewkesbury
Tel: 0684 294516

Telephone enquiries for canal users:
Grand Union (Warwicks) 0926 42192
Staffs and Worcs 02993 77661
Worcester and Birmingham
  Stratford Canal (northern) 0527 72572
  Stratford Canal (southern) 05643 3370
Gloucester-Sharpness 0452 25524

Recorded information for fishermen:
Severn north of Bewdley 0743 8037
Lower Severn and Avon 0684 296929

National Trust:
Head Office:
36 Queen Anne's Gate,
London SW1
Tel: 01 222 9521
Severn Region Office,
34-36 Church Street,
Tewkesbury
Tel: 0684 297747

Camping Club of Great Britain and
Ireland,
11 Lower Grosvener Place,
London SW1W 0EY
Tel: 01 828 1012

Caravan Club,
East Grinstead House,
London Road,
East Grinstead,
Sussex
Tel: 0342 26944

British Canoe Union,
45 High Street,
Addlestone,
Weybridge,
Surrey
Tel: 0932 41341

Cyclists' Touring Club,
69 Meadrow,
Godalming,
Surrey
Tel: 04868 7217

Youth Hostels Association,
Trevelyan House,
St Albans,
Hertfordshire
Tel: 0727 55215

Index